Preface

When they read this book my friends and acquaintances may not immediately recognise it is about me. Many of them will not see that the difficulties I am discussing are mine. Some people think that autism is external, and that it is visible, but they are wrong. Autism is invisible and it may be present without being obvious. It is inside you.

Meanwhile, I have become an expert at hiding difficulties caused by my autism. If there is something I simply can't do, or if I find it very difficult, people around me might not necessarily notice. I know lots of tricks to prevent me from making a poor show, or people noticing my inability to do certain things. My repertoire for solving difficulties is considerable. In fact I have little choice. I look normal, even as a child I looked normal, and therefore I was always expected to fulfil all demands. There was no consideration for my autism. After all, the difficulty didn't exist; it was not visible. It was pointless trying to explain that there was something wrong. I often tried, but as far as everybody else was concerned, there just wasn't anything wrong.

On the outside it looks as if I am quite capable, but people do not realise how much effort it takes for me to perform even the most basic tasks. Nobody knows how exhausting and what a strain it is.

This book was written from one particular stance. I began to write, because I was having a difficult time. I felt writing would help me create clarity for myself – I wanted to understand myself through writing. My book became a report of extensive introspection. It is as if I wanted to list my defects, like a car mechanic with the vehicles in his garage. This made it a rather one-sided report; I did not immediately highlight what went well and to some extent I only portrayed my failures. Nevertheless I still find it difficult to describe my difficulties and failures, and even after you have read this book full of my experiences, you may still not understand how invasive autism is. It may still not be totally clear how I experience things, nor can I fully emphasise how painful and miserable life can be for me, how frustrating it is to see how well others manage in comparison.

I did not intend to write a book. I was just writing for my own benefit, and to clarify my condition to people around me. The experiences, difficulties and problems, which I have described, never quite recur to the same degree. Sometimes they all happen at the same time; sometimes there has been improvement in some, but I have had to face new difficulties with regard to others. However, I do think that this book is an honest reflection of my life.

I am still unable to express myself properly; I cannot yet explain adequately what autism is like for me and what it means to me. I am searching for words, but there don't seem to be any that fit.

Some people don't believe me. My reply is, "Try spending a week with me... you will soon find out!"

Contents

Chapter 1

The Diagnosis

Quite some time ago I constantly had recurrent arguments with Bart, my boyfriend. Often they were about silly things, too silly to argue about. I was always aggressive in my response and I would never give in. It was far too difficult for me to compromise. Although we both realised the root of the difficulties lay somewhere deep down, we couldn't work it out. We reached the point where we began to worry about our relationship. I felt he didn't understand me, and he didn't know how to cope with me. He didn't understand why my responses were so bitchy, and he certainly didn't know how to calm me down. Sometimes his attempts to comfort me had the opposite effect, and everything just got worse. It didn't make sense to either of us.

I felt misunderstood and let down. I felt I was so different and that I spoke another language. What I considered to be important didn't matter to him at all. I was always annoyed because my boyfriend did not understand me and because one argument constantly followed another. It was as if I was on another planet. It looked as if we might have to end our relationship as neither of us were benefiting from it.

I lost my job during that period. When I inquired, I was told that my work as a care worker was good and that they praised me for it, but my relationships with colleagues were so awkward that they felt they would have to dismiss me. They felt that I was a hindrance to the team. My colleagues couldn't understand me, and didn't know what was bothering me. That was when I decided something had to be done about it. I had always enjoyed my work and didn't want this scenario to be repeated in the future.

On the computer I listed all the aspects where I differed from other people. I included instances that didn't seem right or when I suspected other people might have solved them or handled them differently. Many instances involved my boyfriend. Each situation that appeared to affect me in a different way to how others were affected was recorded. My boyfriend began to understand me much better and realised that something was seriously wrong. Eventually the list became such a big pile of papers that I took it to a psychiatrist asking her what the matter was with me. After reading my report the psychiatrist thought it might be autism, but she also said that she was not specialised in autism and did not know enough about it.

My boyfriend and that psychiatrist were the first to take the notion of autism seriously. They felt strongly that it was the correct diagnosis, and I was put in touch with Theo Peeters, who confidently assured me that I suffered from autism. Subsequently, my current psychiatrists confirmed their suspicions.

Theo Peeters and my psychiatrist told me that they were touched by my way of describing my autism. They were not the only ones who were moved; many people who have read my story since have said so too, which has been extremely important to me. It was a sign that something of what I have felt and meant to say has been understood, that my story represents something of what goes on inside me, and that I can explain what life is like for me.

The actual diagnosis is very important to me; autism is part of my identity and therefore it should be recognised. To deny autism is to deny my identity. Only too often have I been confronted with a lack of understanding. As a child and when I was an adolescent I tried to make others see that I was different and even then nobody would believe me. My problems were always swept aside and as far as others were concerned I was a normal, though difficult child.

The diagnosis of autism explains a lot to me and that is helpful. I now understand what has caused a lot of problems, and therefore it is easier for me to deal with them. Situations that used to cause me to panic or be upset, I can now resolve. I no longer wish to ignore myself, which is what others have done frequently. Now I know that I am suffering from autism it explains why I find it so difficult to do certain things and the explanation makes everything more bearable.

The diagnosis has also saved my relationship with my boyfriend. My boyfriend now understands me much better, because he can put many difficulties into context. He has learnt to see the difference between autism and me. It no longer makes him angry when I do something as a result of my autism, because he understands. We can now also talk about it safely. I used to feel he was attacking me when he began to talk about my awkward behaviour. Now we just talk about it and look for solutions to tackle difficulties or how to avoid them.

The diagnosis has actually helped to save other relationships with friends and acquaintances, both far away and nearby, contacts with colleagues in the Scout movement and any organisation of which I am a member. Those people never really understood me either.

The diagnosis gave us an explanation. Finally issues could be discussed. At last the people I mixed with could ask me the questions they had wanted to ask me for some time; now they could express verbally what they had been unable to say previously. When they heard about the diagnosis, they told me that it had opened up a new world to them, and that before they hadn't been able to get on with me nor had they understood how I felt and thought. Thanks to the diagnosis they were able to see everything more clearly. Suddenly there was openness and scope for dialogue in relationships that had been difficult or beyond restoration. Moreover, people showed considerable understanding, or at least the potential to understand, instead of continually reproaching and arguing. They showed interest and wondered how I managed, instead of simply calling me unmanageable or awkward. The false accusations had stopped – that is how I had always regarded their reproaches.

In spite of the diagnosis I will still continue to be different. Nobody will ever quite understand me, nor will I understand them. I will continue my struggle to try and conform as much as possible. In that respect nothing has changed since the diagnosis;

my fight requires a great deal of effort. I think it is quite a natural, healthy struggle to survive. The diagnosis has not prevented me from trying to conform or trying to be like other people. I will continue to put a lot of effort into it, because it is my choice to do so. Fortunately my being different has become more accepted, which makes me feel more accepted by others. The diagnosis has made me more self-assured. The majority of people certainly don't respond in this manner, but friends and acquaintances around me are showing willingness. And they, however few, are the ones that matter. They used to judge me by what they saw, without really listening to me as a person, to who I am, to what I feel and think. They showed no interest in my wishes and desires, nor did they ask me any questions, in short they simply ignored me. Now people dare to ask me questions, I have become more than just a shy, closed person.

A lot of people cannot accept the diagnosis. After all, I went on to further education and completed my course with a diploma, I am a Scout Group leader, I have friends, even a boyfriend, I talk to people, I am not afraid of people – so how could I possibly be autistic? They see me as someone trying to discover herself, someone who has got herself into a mess, who is depressed, too critical of herself... Many people only see what I can do successfully: they only see me at work in the house, or at Scouts, in other words, in places where I feel at ease and at home. And these are the environments where they might not notice anything unusual about me. The difficulties are inside me, but they don't understand. However, I am fully aware of them, they never go away, they are part of me, and they are always with me, wherever I go. This kind of misunderstanding and disbelief hurts me. Most people don't like talking about it, whereas open discussion can be so healing. I will go on fighting. I want people to accept me as I am. I am fed up of having to push myself to my limits in order to hide my difficulties and to compensate for them in order to be like everybody else.

All my life I have tried to show something was wrong, and yet nobody has been prepared to listen. I have been bumping my head against a brick wall, and I have found it impossible to make a breakthrough. Time and time again, I have met with the same disbelief. Again and again, I am confronted with the taboo surrounding me, the taboo that there is nothing wrong, that I am just a difficult, unmanageable and stubborn person, while everybody pretty well knows that something is seriously wrong with me. They do talk about it, but among themselves instead of to me. Even my classmates at nursery knew about it: Dominique is different. I was always told to stop being awkward, and that it was time I adopted standard behaviour.

I would love to behave like most other people, but I find it impossible. Even if I wanted to – and I do 300% – I just can't. The natural order of society doesn't make sense to me at all, and it shows in tiny details. They tell me that I am not the centre of the world and that it is up to me to conform, because the world certainly won't change to suit me. Actually, all my life I have been fully aware of the fact that I am outside the world, in other words, I am not part of it. This is the crux of the matter, because from the moment I wake up in the morning, I try to conform and behave in the way any other person would. Meanwhile, I would love to disappear and merge with the crowds – how I hate being different, not being invisible. I cannot conform, and I will never be able to, not even to my dying day. I am different and always will be and all I can do is cover up and pretend there is no difference. I try very hard to conform, but the harder I try, the more I succeed (although only externally), and the more exhausted and unaccepted I feel. The more effort I put into it, the greater and more painful the contrast appears to me. I try to live up to the expectations of other people because it is easier for them, if I appear to be less different. If I am more like them I am less of a nuisance, however my true self becomes suppressed. I cannot be who I want to be; I have always hidden my true nature. I was always given the blame and therefore I believed it was me who was wrong. Sometimes I was ashamed of myself and I wanted to hide because I felt worthless. I was always on guard, thinking nobody wanted me.

I don't blame anyone. My handicap was invisible; nobody knew I was autistic, but I still suffer the consequences. I still have an indistinct feeling that I am not allowed to be who I want to be, which bothers me, even today. When I act in an unusual manner, I still dare not explain that it is because of my autism – I still think I am not allowed to be that way; I am still ashamed and I automatically hide myself. Before I can talk about it, I need to overcome several hurdles and convince myself that I can do it. Even when surrounded by people who entirely accept me and my autism, I will still spontaneously efface myself – a typical response, which is firmly embedded.

I often conflict with people because I respond and act differently as a result of my autism, but I cannot explain to them what has caused my strange behaviour. When they think I have done something wrong, they are cross with me and if I were to explain the reason, in other words, my autism, it would feel as if I were trying to talk myself out of it. I don't want to use my autism as an excuse. Consequently it leaves me as the guilty party, which to me is preferable to any attempt to save face. Very often it is quite easy to explain why I do or don't do certain things and conflicts could be resolved quite quickly if I were to indicate which actions are impossible because of my autism, but I can't. I am too afraid that others will think I am using autism to justify myself.

As a child I often tried to explain what had happened and I would always get the same response: that I was being silly or that I was lying. Nobody would listen to me. When I tried to tell them I was unable to do something, or tried to indicate a difficulty, my difficulties were swept aside and they would not take me seriously. Today I still don't dare to explain in case I might be reproached. I prefer to be considered guilty rather than be rejected.

Now I know I am autistic, I want to tell everybody what it is like for me to be autistic. I want everybody to know that some things are impossible for me to do and that it isn't a matter of unwillingness. Moreover, I want everybody to let me be who I am, without wishing to change me. Each time I tell somebody that I am autistic I have to fight my inhibitions and my knees are shaking with fear that they may not believe me. And yet I choose to tell them, even though they sometimes look at me incredulously and claim I can't possibly be autistic. Too many people have a very stereotypical picture of autism.

Now that I am able to explain how difficulties manifest themselves, many people try to offer solutions as if I am presenting a minor problem that can be resolved. They often do not understand the impact of autism, which makes me feel extremely unhappy and hurt because I long to be understood. Meanwhile, I do realise that it is partly my fault and that I still don't know how to explain adequately what my autism means. And of course they, too, need time to understand, which I need to give them. I generally do listen although some days, when I am not feeling too well, it is more difficult and I become angry. All they need to do is listen. After all, I am the one who has to live with it.

Talks

I have also been giving talks about my autism, which are very important to me. There is enough time and space during those talks to tell my story as comprehensively as possible and I love the attention. On those occasions my audience always believe me. They allow me to say all I want to say and to be clear. Unfortunately most people have the wrong picture of autism. They expect 'autistics' (I hate that word) to be trapped within themselves, unable to communicate in any way.

That is why I want to write and give talks so that my audience will also hear about other types of autistics. I want them to know that people with autism aren't necessarily like their stereotypical image. We may even appear to be normal people, and I would like them to understand that autism happens within and not externally. It would be great if they saw the other side of autism and forgot their original idea.

I know that the false picture causes many people to disbelieve me. I hope they will be able to put that picture aside and be willing to observe how autism affects me. I cannot blame them for being uninformed, I just hope that they will look and try to understand. Even my GP would not believe me because he was hooked on a stereotypical image. When I told him about my diagnosis his response was that ideally I should forget about it as quickly as possible; he advised me not to believe it. After all, I could look into his eyes and I wasn't banging my head on the table, so I couldn't possibly be autistic! I have never known such shortsightedness.

My GP immediately gave me a sick-note. I needed a good rest, which would make me feel better and help me to look at the situation from a different perspective. He wanted me to feel better. Why? I had just begun to feel great. I felt fantastic and didn't need a rest at all. I had plenty of energy, because after 24 years I had finally discovered what the matter was with me, I had found answers to all my questions and difficulties and I had discovered my own identity.

I told a couple of friends about my autism. I had feared they would not understand or believe me, which was true initially. Understanding often doesn't come until they have read this story, or until they have received some additional explanation. I often find myself sitting at a table with a captivated, interested audience listening to my story, and it really does me a world of good to find people prepared to listen, particularly because they are listening to me and my story and hearing about my true self. They are fascinated and after all I have been through, this gives me a great sense of satisfaction.

Generally, my friends show some understanding for which I am grateful. They realise my difficulties, which is a great achievement, time and time again. This feeling of acceptance is fantastic. However, there are people who are very important to me (such as my family) who prefer to push my diagnosis aside, which hurts. I have had to give my parents time in order to come to terms with the diagnosis. They still find it difficult, but they are trying. It is not easy to be told after many years that your daughter is autistic, and maybe they will never fully accept it. Nevertheless, I have noticed that they are trying to show interest when I am about to give a talk or working on matters with regard to autism. And that is all I expect from them; they need not accept it entirely, they need not completely put up with it, I just want them to let it be there, to not mind me talking about it when I want to and to not disbelieve me or reject the diagnosis.

When I first told them about the diagnosis they said they never wanted to hear the word autism again, which was a bold statement that hurt me deeply. They have come a long way and they should feel proud.

E.T.

During a course for people with autism I had a moving experience. All the participants were young adults. They were intelligent and had been to mainstream schools; they had been to further and higher education and lived independently. All my doubts disappeared after that two-day course, which made me feel stronger and self-assured. The course helped me to accept my autism and I felt just like E.T. who had finally arrived on his own planet.

When I first attended the course I had known about my autism for less than a month and I had not quite come to terms with it. I couldn't yet quite comprehend it because it was too great a concept. Actually, I was still in the denial phase. Sometimes I recognised I was autistic and other times I just couldn't accept it and I wished it weren't true. However, I recognised myself in all those young people I met during the two-day course.

At first I was quite scared. I had decided that there were two possibilities: either I would be faced with the fact that I really was autistic and life would be difficult, or I would turn out not to be autistic at all, which would upset me too. In some ways those young people with autism were copies of me; the similarities struck me. For the first time in my life I felt at home and after the second day I didn't want to leave, because I didn't want to lose the wonderful feeling inside me. The mentor told me I looked radiantly happy. When I arrived home that evening, I cried for hours and realised I had never before felt at ease and that there had never been a place where I had felt as happy as on the course. I realised that I had never fully understood the word acceptance until now. I knew this special feeling had been lacking all my life and I realised that I had not even noticed something essential was missing. It was clearly something that was natural to others.

During the course I was also deeply struck by the fact that people with autism are very capable. Initially my parents didn't accept my autism because I have quite good social skills, but during the course I noticed that when it comes to social behaviour I am at the lower end of the scale. Even I appeared to have had a stereotypical picture of autism, which was now gone. I saw that people with autism could address and talk to others and that they could even have group discussions. Most importantly I realised that autism just didn't show in many of them, that they could live in society without others initially noticing any difference. During any brief encounter they might appear rather quiet or shy, but generally people will not realise anything is amiss, until they really get to know them, such as in my case.

The two-day course was quite a revelation. I wish I could have filmed the experience to be able to show it to all my disbelievers, to show them that there are lots of people with autism who look just like me and are equally capable.

Now, much later, I have a clearer picture of what we cannot do. I increasingly notice that there are lots of things I can't do or do differently. There are lots of things I thought I could do, but I was wrong. The puzzle has not yet been completed, because each day I notice new difficulties related to my autism – difficulties I tend to cover up or resolve in another way. I thought everybody resolved them in the same way, but that was a misconception. Consequently, I hardly doubt the diagnosis, as everything is becoming much clearer. I can now see things I was not prepared to see previously.

(W)underway (a leisure organisation for people with autism) gave me my second important experience. I can't quite put into words what happened to me, but when I go to the meetings, particularly our Friday evening group meetings, I experience many emotions. Once again if feels like an 'E.T. coming home' experience, because I am given the recognition that has been lacking all my life. I don't have to stay on an alien planet, no; I can go to my own planet. Since I got to know (W)underway I continually want to 'go home', to the 'right planet.' I finally know what it feels like to be at home. I didn't previously know what it felt like, I didn't have a place I could call my own, I felt as if I didn't belong to this earth, this planet.

(W)underway is my home. (W)underway is what home should be like. It is where I can recuperate, where I feel good, where I do not happen to be a counter magnet. (W)underway fills me with a strong feeling of acceptance and recognition.

It was as if I had been given a lifelong sentence at birth. My diagnosis means I feel acquitted, personally, with regards to my boyfriend and my psychiatrist. I will have to go through the same process again with all other people, because that is what it feels like to me – a court case. The only difference is that I was guilty from the very beginning and had to prove my innocence.

Having won my case once isn't enough. I need to be acquitted by the whole world, or at least by my world. Everybody has given me a life sentence, which means I have to replicate my case in front of everybody, case by case, person by person. Surely we don't all have to fight so hard to survive?

Writing

Since I have been given the diagnosis I have noticed more autistic traits in myself than I previously suspected. Small things I used to think were a little odd, I now relate to autism. Before I was given the diagnosis I had no choice but to ignore them. I couldn't attend to them in the way I needed to and everything remained difficult. I couldn't allow myself to try and resolve small difficulties and it troubled me that they made life so awkward. I blamed myself and was unfair to myself out of ignorance. Now I am happy because my awareness helps me to clear minor difficulties; small issues that used to bother me no longer do. Nor do I become irritable, because I know what causes it, and now that many difficulties are resolved it takes longer before I reach the point where I can't cope. My frustration level is higher. Of course it can sometimes be discouraging to see how some small matters don't simply disappear, while someone else could not imagine that they might even cause a problem.

Writing can simplify matters, too. It gives me a better understanding and I can channel a lot of the anger, which used to arise from a lack of understanding and not being able to cope with the chaos. On the other hand it can make things more difficult; I am now aware of things I am doing wrong (I would say, differently), where I used to think I was managing quite well. Consequently some areas are increasingly becoming a chore. I have now discovered autism is responsible for limitations at Scouts where I thought I displayed considerably less autistic behaviour. For instance, in the hut there are many different types of coffee spoons and I always want one particular spoon. It is very important to me, while others don't realise that the wrong spoon can ruin my whole evening. I used to think I was silly getting so worked up about a spoon, but now I know what is causing it I can make my evening run smoothly by making sure that I can use my spoon. I can now pre-empt my frustrations and avoid them, which helps my self-image. I used to find myself very awkward and highly inflammable. I used to be cross with myself and often hated myself. I saw myself as an intolerant, finicky person. I wanted to change myself and became increasingly angry when I wasn't successful, and of course I didn't succeed! I know now that it is not related to me as a person, and therefore I don't look at myself in the same negative light and I can frequently resolve the issue.

I still find it difficult to ask for help. It is not easy for me to indicate when I need help and what kind I need. This is because I haven't quite come to terms with the diagnosis, which came rather late. Nobody knows how much energy it requires and how hard I try. If they had known I was autistic, they would have been able to teach me how to ask for help, whereas I was assumed to be quite capable of doing everything myself like anybody else. Of course I couldn't and consequently people were disappointed in me. They didn't understand and got angry, or would reproach me or tell me I was putting it on. Therefore I still can't indicate what I need, which is a nuisance. It is embedded in me that I should be able to do everything like anybody else and that I shouldn't ask for help because people will frown. I continually feel the pressure to fulfil all demands.

Chapter 2

Difficulties in Everyday Life

I drive a car and I use public transport. I know the Highway Code and to all appearances I can get around quite well. I can find my way almost anywhere, but it requires an enormous amount of effort; nobody could imagine to what extent because all they see is that I reach my destinations.

Of course I know the traffic signs, but I often don't see them. I only see them when they are in regular places and even then I might miss them. If a traffic sign is in an unusual position, I can't accept that the light or sign applies to me. If it were meant for me it would be in another position, wouldn't it? Therefore, I will continue without stopping, even if it is a red light, I will turn into one-way streets against the flow, or not follow a sign to 'Antwerp' when I am on my way there. I do this when the signs present themselves in an unexpected or unusual position, and because I haven't seen them there before, I can't accept their authenticity. My mind wants everything to be the same; it can't accept change. It doesn't even occur to me to consider change.

Recently a Scout leader and I were looking for a site for a Scout weekend camp. Suddenly we reached a peculiar junction. I had never seen one like it before. When I approached it – very slowly – I saw the lights had changed to red. The traffic lights were however in an unusual position and didn't seem right. They should be somewhere else, so I concluded that they were not meant for me and therefore I didn't stop. The Scout leader was amazed. He asked me what I was doing and found my explanation quite amusing.

I can read street names, a map and a town plan yet I can often not find my way. I have such a poor sense of direction that I don't know how to use a road map. I can't even use a road map on an estate where I know several streets.

The same route

I always choose the same route to go somewhere and as a result I don't see how different streets relate to each other. I have no difficulty walking from my house to my local supermarket, nor walking from my house to Aldi. I know all the streets between my supermarket and Aldi, but I can't find my way on foot from the local supermarket to Aldi. I first need to go back to my house, even though it lengthens my journey. I just wouldn't know how to walk directly from my supermarket to Aldi. I simply don't have any sense of direction. It means my journeys often take much longer. I can find my way around in Antwerp, but it can take me half an hour to get from one shop to the next. When I finally reach the second shop I notice that it is just around the corner from the first shop and that it should have taken me no more than three minutes. I cannot use a map or a town plan, they are too abstract, and I just can't visualise the actual streets. If I know the area well, I might be able to recognise a few things on a road map.

Of course it isn't difficult to stop someone and ask the way, but the directions are of little use to me. They are too abstract, which means I cannot visualise what has been said and therefore I cannot remember. I can manage as far as two turnings but that is my limit, because I can't make a mental picture. I can only use the directions if I know the area well, so that I know where each step will take me. Even then they should not be too complicated and it will only work if they cover a short distance. Even if I know the route well, having been there many times, I still can't picture it. I may not know what hides behind the corner, although I have been there hundreds of times. I will only know when I actually turn the corner, regardless of whether I have been there previously. I can only picture what is round the corner in my immediate surroundings, where I have lived all my life. Further on it will be totally new to me, which actually prevents me going somewhere. I don't know how to continue until I am actually there, which is why I can't see how my regular venues relate to each other, not even in my own town where I know every street.

Small details help me to remember my route, but I do not have them at my fingertips. For instance, when I visit my friend, I always turn off when I see a particular dustbin. Therefore, if the dustbin has been moved, I am lost and I can no longer remember the way from that junction onwards. It is hard to tell if the missing dustbin causes my difficulty. It simply means that when given directions, I can't imagine where the end of a road leads to, even though I may have been down the road a number of times.

I don't have any sense of direction at all. Even inside buildings I can't find my bearings. I can't even usually remember the way to the exit. At the end of my first visit to somebody in a flat, I am often confused and can't find the external door, which really bothers me. At home I couldn't tell you which room is under my bedroom, because I just can't picture it, even though I have lived there for 22 years. My family do not understand. They have been trying to tell me which window corresponds with the window on the floor below or above, and that the garden wall in my bedroom corresponds with the kitchen wall adjoining the garden on the ground floor. I really don't understand and therefore I have simply memorised it without comprehending.

I will never drive on routes I have not tried before. I have a set number of venues I go to: Scouts, my grandparents and some friends. I never drive anywhere else. If I really need to go somewhere new, I will first travel with my boyfriend and be the passenger a couple of times and then my boyfriend will accompany me several times, while I drive. Finally I will have a try on my own. But I have rarely added a new venue to my list: the resistance I feel is too great.

On the road

When I go somewhere with my boyfriend, I need to be absolutely sure which route he is going to take. If he does not tell me beforehand, I am difficult to get on with. Those are the moments when we often have a row in the car, because the whole situation becomes unmanageable for me. For instance, going on to the motorway without any pre-warning is impossible, I just can't do it. I hate certain roads or streets and very often I refuse to go down them. Therefore, I usually ask my boyfriend not to go down those streets when I am his passenger.

Sometimes when I am travelling with my boyfriend I get very upset. If he takes another route to the one I am used to or the one I had in mind, it can suddenly make me very angry or unreasonable. To me it is very important and it is something I like to know beforehand. Taking another route makes a big difference to me; it creates an awful lot of resistance in me and makes me feel impotent.

The fact that I never drive on my own to a new destination is a serious handicap when I meet with roadworks. If I happen to be on my own, I will turn back. When my boyfriend is with me I might continue, if he does not want to take over, but I will begin to panic and I get very angry. He needs to give me very clear instructions and be careful that I do not explode. On such occasions I become a very unpleasant person and extremely upset. The same problems may recur if a flower trough or an advertising board has been moved. If a diversion takes a long time, I will again feel resistance when the diversion has ended. I can't get myself to take the usual road.

If it is very busy I am likely to have difficulties on my usual daily routes. An unusual manoeuvre in traffic will cause me to panic. If a car in front of me disobeys the traffic rules, or acts contrary to expectations, I simply don't know how to respond. It makes me uncertain and my behaviour becomes unpredictable. I don't see the danger and a wrong response could make me an even greater hazard. Often I don't know what to do and I freeze; I refuse to continue. My day is ruined and I feel shattered.

When it is busy on the road there are too many stimuli for me to cope with; everything is happening too quickly and I tend to become panicky. I refuse to drive during peak hours or when it is busy. You will never see me in the city where it is crowded and if I end up in a queue I refuse to continue.

If I happen to see a traffic warden directing the traffic, I don't know what to do. I don't understand their signals and I am never quite sure if I should continue or stop or take another road.

I tend not to go on bus or tramlines that are unfamiliar to me; I will only travel on regular routes. I will usually get on and off at the same stop, even if it means a long walk. If I need to go somewhere I have not been to before, I can't take a tram or a bus. If I do, it will create a lot of resistance in me and I will need very clear directions. I will feel extremely tense.

Making phone calls

I don't find it difficult to make phone calls and yet they can be a source of frustration. A call is always unexpected, which is something I find very difficult. It unnerves me because I want to plan everything. If I had planned to read a book and there is a phone call, or the phone rings while I am washing up, it upsets me. I also like to know beforehand what kind of call it is likely to be, how long the phone call will last and what we will be talking about, which of course is not very realistic. It can make phoning an unpleasant activity. If the call doesn't run the way I had planned it to go, my feeling of panic might make me sound very unfriendly. I don't have any difficulty with short business calls, such as arranging dates, because they are clearly defined, but if someone rings me for a chat it is a little harder and makes me feel uncomfortable. When people ring for a chat, they often cover lots of different topics or tell bits of news. If I do not know the subject beforehand, I feel resistance rising up in me.

I always arrange with my boyfriend when to call each other, which makes it more predictable. I can become fraught if he rings early or late. Therefore I prefer to ring people myself, instead of being called by them, because then I can at least determine the time. If I decide to call someone for seven minutes and it takes longer I tend to be abrupt, but if people want to put the phone down sooner than anticipated, I try to prolong the call so that I can end it myself when the seven minutes are up. If my caller raises an unexpected subject I am ill at ease. The call has to go according to my expectations. My boyfriend knows and complies. Sometimes I am unmanageable during a call. He then tells me that he will ring back at a certain time for about a quarter of an hour, which makes me happy.

Watching television

Watching television can be difficult. I don't understand the jokes. I get on quite well with informative programmes, but all the information needs to be truthful. Therefore chat programmes tend to irritate me. Sometimes they tell jokes during the discussions or the guests try to evade the truth or tell us things that are clearly lies. Everybody else realises what's going on, except me. I will then tell those jokes to other people, believing them to be true. I can't stand cartoons; they are far too quick. There are too many flashing pictures and I don't understand the fantasy. I like to watch a film but I prefer not to talk about it. I find it difficult to follow a film and usually I don't grasp the plot; I generally disagree with the ending. Tragedies and true stories are easier for me to understand.

Meals

I can't cook, because I can't manage two things at the same time. I can either prepare potatoes or vegetables, or meat. There will be times that I merely eat potatoes without anything else; occasionally I will enjoy meat or vegetables, but never the three combined. I can't keep an eye on more than one pan at a time. I now go to cookery classes where they give us plans intended for people with autism. They tell us step by step what needs to be done. It means that I never have to deal with two things at the same time and it makes cooking feasible. Everything is subdivided into small manageable steps. Therefore I can manage, although I don't have an overview of what is happening, and that is why I can't anticipate what still needs doing. I can't deviate from the plan; on the contrary I follow it rigidly.

My meals are not varied. There are times that I can't eat anything but pizza, and I will eat pizza only for several days in a row. There was a time that I never ate sandwiches, and there are frequent periods that I still can't eat any sandwiches. I will only eat sandwich filling if it was bought the same day and only immediately after purchase. I can't leave it lying around for even an hour. If I would like another cheese sandwich several hours after lunch, it is impossible because it is too long after I bought the food. One hour after purchase the remaining sandwich spreads will be chucked in the bin.

Nor can I reheat foods. If there are some leftovers after I have cooked potatoes, I will not be able to eat them the next day. The same applies to my pizza binges; if I stop for half an hour, I will not be able to continue eating my pizza.

I will only eat fruit on the day it is bought; in fact this applies to all foods. The only exception is pop such as fizzy lemonade, but then I need to finish the lemonade or a similar drink completely, before I can drink anything else. And thus I often don't drink what I feel like. However, this does not apply to fizzy mineral water and fruit juices.

I miss many meals. Sometimes I only have one a day. There are many days that I don't eat at all. Usually I only have one cooked meal per day and nothing else and that meal can be at any time between 11 o'clock in the morning and midnight.

I can't make my own decision about what to have for dinner. My boyfriend always does that for me. For a little while we tried a different approach: he would set up a menu at the beginning of the week, but our discussion led to a lot of resistance and arguments. I can't approve just any menu; there is always some kind of resistance in me. Often I can't keep myself to the agreement and I need my boyfriend to help me change it. Changing something just like that upsets my plan and I feel hopelessly lost. My eating difficulties make me want to ring my boyfriend at the most impossible moments. And yet, if I go out for a meal they disappear. My eating difficulties didn't really emerge until I left home. Sometimes they become a bit too extreme; the problem has grown out of proportion, requiring too much energy and making me feel too much resistance.

I have other kinds of difficulty in other places, because I associate certain restaurants with certain dishes. There is one venue where I can only eat lasagne, and another where I can only eat a toasted ham-and-cheese sandwich, and somewhere else I can only choose a salmon dish. It is very annoying but I can't get away from it. Even if I don't really feel like that particular dish at that particular moment, I will still take it. It doesn't occur to me that I could choose something else; it would be out of the question. Usually I can't even make a choice. What is the right moment to eat steak, rabbit or fish? Due to these eating difficulties I can suffer from a shortage of vitamins.

Shopping

I find shopping difficult. If I have a list, everything on that list has to be available in the shop; otherwise I will panic and give up shopping. On another occasion it will take hours to shop if there is something missing on the list, or if I can't find the right brand. My usual brands have to be there, and in the right place, otherwise I won't find them. If a shop repeatedly changes its interior, which means all the products have been moved, I give up shopping. I will be at my wit's end and I will leave the shop immediately with no desire to continue. A few days later I will go back to the shop to have a look around, without buying anything just to find out where they have put everything. Once I know where everything is, I will attempt another visit with a shopping list.

I can only go shopping if I have a list, otherwise I don't know what I need to buy and I get confused. A list, however, means that everything has to be selected before I can leave the shop. It is not possible for me to enter a new shop. I have my regular shops and I can't deviate. I will never go to another baker, so if my baker's is closed I just won't eat. If they don't have my brand of milk, I won't have any milk. It is very difficult for me to add new shops to my list and I certainly can't do it on my own. My boyfriend needs to be with me. Such a day is very difficult for me and it will take me considerable time to recover.

Some shops I will visit by car, others on foot. It is a habit I can't change, not even if I unexpectedly need to buy many items for a party, or if I only need to buy one thing. I will only travel by car if there is a parking space, which means only shops with big car parks are eligible. Nor can I decide whether I am going to visit a new shop by car or on foot; once again my boyfriend will have to help me decide.

I have sharp eyes, but if they have changed the packaging I won't be able to find the items. I don't recognise the products and therefore I'm not sure if I am looking at the right ones. If a product has been moved somewhere else along the shelves it unsettles me and I may be walking up and down the same aisle ten times to find it. I know it should be there and yet I can't find it, which is extremely frustrating and many people don't understand. Often I ask the shop assistants to help me, but if I ask them where to find the chocolate, they will only point towards the aisle, and if I tell them that I can't find it there, they respond with incredibly little understanding. They might say that it must be out of stock or that I haven't looked properly. It isn't easy, having to ask repeatedly if they will go with me and show me, as if I am asking too much. There is such a lack of understanding, while it must be a common problem. It makes me feel quite tense each time I need to go to the shop.

If there isn't a price on the products, I may wonder if it is for sale; it confuses me when the price is below, or on the shelf, or on the product itself. I am not sure if the price belongs to the box or the packet; it is difficult for me to believe that the price belongs to the product. I also have difficulties finding the sell-by date and I am always wondering if it is correct.

It is hard for me to find my way around supermarkets. If I have chosen to shop in my local supermarket, I can't possibly go to another branch. I often can't even find the exit in a new shop, or the checkouts. I will have to ask and then I do not understand the explanation because it is too vague.

I can't decide whether I should wear warm or light clothing. I need to be told when to change into my winter coat. The first year I was living on my own I walked around without a coat till December, because nobody had told me I needed to change into a winter coat.

I can't co-ordinate clothes. I just can't see which items match and therefore I always wear the same jumper with the same trousers, and never in any other combination. When I go and buy clothes, I will always buy a pair of trousers and a sweater at the same time;

otherwise I don't know how to match them. If someone gives me a sweater, I won't wear it because there isn't a pair of trousers to go with it.

I always buy my clothes in the same shop. Most importantly, the assistants should be clear in their explanations. Buying clothes is surrounded by tension due to all the difficulties that may arise. It takes a long time; I can't make any decision on my own because I can't judge if it is the right one. I will decide beforehand what I am going to buy, because I can't make choices. If my boyfriend points out to me that there happens to be something else in a much more attractive colour, I will not be able to buy it because I hadn't planned to. I can't then buy the original colour I had intended to buy, because it no longer feels right. There are so many other and more attractive items in the shop.

Visiting the doctor

Very often I don't go to my GP in time. I always leave the practice without having discussed what I originally went for. I can't really tell whether I am sick or not, nor do I realise the degree of my illness. If I think I have a throat infection, I might be told I have an inflammation of the stomach or a bladder infection, which I hadn't noticed. When I am ill I think I am not ill enough and that I need to wait a little longer before I go. Meanwhile the illness has got considerably worse. I hardly ever go to the GP of my own accord; my boyfriend will advise me.

Housework

I tend to have quite a few problems doing housework, I can only do something when it has been planned, but at the same time I find it difficult to make plans. If I have little time, I find it easy to make plans. I will just do what needs to be done in the short time I am free, but if I am out of work or have a lot of free time it is a disaster. I just don't know how to plan: what would be the right moment to do the dishes, to clean, to do the washing...? I really don't know where to begin. If I were to decide that I wanted to do something that wasn't planned, I couldn't do it either.

I have similar problems tidying up. If a piece of paper has been lying in the same place for two days – even if it is on the floor – it will be very difficult for me to pick it up and put it in a new place.

Chapter 3

Sensory Stimuli

One of the difficulties caused by my autism is connected with sensory perception. It causes serious disadvantages to me and unfortunately there is very little that can be done about it. It is very annoying because it affects me every moment of the day.

The world often scares me because all my sensory perceptions enter at once. They all come in at the same time and I simply can't differentiate. One stimulus can be so overpowering that I can no longer concentrate on other things. I need all my concentration for one type of stimulus or for one particular stimulus, so that I can't pay any attention at all to all the others. However, if I don't pay any attention to the other stimuli, the rate at which they arrive creates chaos and I can no longer cope. The different aspects reinforce each other, the entire situation is out of control and the best thing for me to do is to extricate myself from that particular situation, because if I don't, I begin to panic or my temper flares up. It also exhausts me and requires an awful lot of energy. In some cases I will lose all my energy within five minutes, because I can't handle the number of stimuli all at once.

Crowds and meeting people

It often happens in a packed hall, a big shop or a crowded tram. A packed hall can be noisy, which I find overpowering. Moreover, people are too close to me. There might be a smell of food or perfume, and possibly buzzing strip lights. Usually it is the noise that hits me, because I find it the most painful. When I am in that packed hall, the noise will envelop me in such a way that I can no longer concentrate on the light or the smells, which in turn will hit me even harder. My feelings at that point can best be described as a survival instinct. I really think I won't be able to cope and if something doesn't happen very quickly everything will go wrong. I panic. The need to escape from that particular situation is the one that drives me. At the same time I feel extremely powerless and can't stand it any longer. I feel like a bomb, ready to explode. It is a horrible, overpowering feeling, which leaves me at my wit's end; nobody should cross my path, because I will be blunt and abrupt. I become extremely unpleasant and have only one aim – to escape from that situation as quickly as possible. All other matters are secondary.

My difficulties with sensory perception are quite extreme and there is not much I can do about them. All I can do is try to avoid situations where I am likely to be confronted with many stimuli, but I can't possibly avoid all of them and of course they recur daily. After all, you can't close your senses down. You can't turn them off, can you? They are very sensitive, and the stimuli are invasive; they cause many of the difficulties with regard to my autism. I can, however, manage if I am distracted, or if I can actually concentrate on something else, or occupy myself otherwise, but this requires all my attention.

It is difficult for me to enter crowded areas, because I don't have a clear overview. It means I often don't dare to enter. This lack of an overview takes control of me. Even more perceptions crowd in together, leading to even more chaos. I see all kinds of things, but can't identify them. I hear sounds that I can't place because of the chaos; simple sounds are beyond recognition due to the high number of impressions. I smell things that I can't recognise, whereas I generally have a sharp scent and can identify many smells. I am afraid of going in, because I don't know if I will manage. I may prefer to stay at the side or sit down. I'm afraid of ending up in the middle of the busyness, without anything to hold onto. I don't mean this it literally, such as being able to sit down or lean against a wall, I mean it metaphorically. At such moments, if I can no longer cope, I really need someone I know or can trust, who knows me and whom I can ask for help.

Unfortunately, I feel more afraid of meeting people socially in those circumstances. It is difficult to analyse social encounters in a busy environment. Meeting people is more confusing than ever, because I am less able to attach any meaning or to interpret what is going on correctly. Busyness makes me feel very unsure, and my generally poor level of coping drops even more. The fear of losing face is greater than ever, because I know from experience it is likely to happen. On such occasions there is no time for socialising. I need so much concentration to cope with impressions that I have no power or energy left to talk to anybody. It can even be too great an effort to greet somebody, which complicates the situation even more.

I regularly suffer from migraines. The headaches are caused by stimuli I cannot deal with. I'm sensitive to flashes of light, strip lights, certain odours, noises, and a rapid succession of visual images, such as cartoons or visually busy programmes. They are too much for me and give me a splitting headache or make me feel nauseous, or sometimes both. I need to be able to rest instantaneously and sleep is the best remedy. When I am tired I'm much more susceptible to headaches. Physically I suffer considerably from not being able to handle sensory stimuli, which is why I cannot work full days. I can't be active all day, because my senses will then create too many difficulties and make me ill. I need rest, not only at night-time, but also during the day.

It was even worse when I was a child, simply because I perceived things differently to other children. I knew my perception was different, but I couldn't put words to it. I visited several doctors who tested my balance, took an EEG, did numerous different scans and sent me to see an ENT consultant. There was a battery of tests, which didn't produce any results.

Everybody around me thought I was too self-critical and that I raised the alarm at the slightest thing. They couldn't find anything wrong and yet I was always complaining. I couldn't manage to convey there was something seriously wrong. At that time nobody believed me and consequently I began to doubt and to believe that I must be exaggerating. As a result I frequently ignored many of the signals and didn't take a rest when my body told me I needed it. As a child and adolescent I just carried on because everybody told me that that was the way. I wanted to live up to their standards and continually overstepped my limits. I ignored the signals, the pain, and the inconvenience. I was often ill, but even then, I didn't allow myself enough rest, because I was fed up with being told that I gave up too quickly. I wanted to be strong, but my responses led to prolonged illnesses. I was more often sick than healthy, but often I didn't let on.

I am happy that I can now say something is wrong and that the problem has always been there, but that you simply can't measure it. I am happy that there is an explanation, I am happy that I now have the confirmation that I haven't been too self-critical, but that there certainly were issues which were difficult for me to handle. Now I am better at listening to my body and I rest when it is necessary and I will even pay attention to the pain I experience when I am inundated by too many stimuli. I also have a mattress in the corner of my living room and I frequently use it during the day. I cannot rest in bed during the day, because a bed is to sleep in at night and therefore I can't lie down on it during daytime. In my vocabulary sleeping is a night-time activity, so what I do during the day is resting or napping, but not sleeping. Since I have had the mattress in my living room and have allowed myself to take a rest during the day I'm coping much better; I really need it.

I regularly visit the psychiatrist, usually during the day. Once we had arranged an appointment at nine o'clock in the evening and it was dark. When I stepped into the hall, I became confused because everything was different, all the colours were different, and I found it difficult to recognise anything. I didn't feel at ease at all, and when I entered the psychiatrist's office, my confusion grew: I had a good look round and yet there were many things I didn't recognise. I was upset and couldn't imagine that the darkness outside was the sole reason. I tried to think of what might have changed and felt like asking if there were new pictures on the wall. I felt awful. Then the psychiatrist told me that she had painted the hallway. I observed all the colours and realised that I hadn't noticed. I told her everything looked different and felt overcome by impotence when I heard myself telling her, because I realised that it was quite abnormal. It was too confrontational to hear myself making those statements. My whole life I had tried to hide the issue and even look for answers, but had never succeeded. When it is dark I try to avoid going to places that I normally visit during the day, because it is too confusing. I can't cope, because I can't recognise anything.

I still don't understand mirror images, which has obviously caused considerable difficulties while driving. When I look in my rear mirror and a see the car behind me indicating to go left, I never know which turn it will take. If there are a man and woman in the car behind me, I can never tell who is sitting on the right or on the left. But also during bongo or dancing lessons, or Tai Ji, it can be a nuisance. It used to bother me at school during lessons in art and technology and while doing practical work. When I am shown how to do something today, I usually can't copy. When my teacher stood in front of me and showed me an exercise, I couldn't even repeat the easiest of exercises, and I still can't, because it is a mirror image. It makes no sense to me, I can't analyse the movements or make sense of them. If you want to show me something, you should stand next to me, or even better stand in front of me with your back towards me, which makes it much clearer. If you then raise your hand, I will see immediately which hand it is. This is why I have not been able to learn many things.

Hot and cold

My perception of hot and cold isn't straightforward either. When I test the temperature of the bathwater, I use my hands as I can feel fairly accurately with them. But when I get into the bath my feet really hurt and at that moment I can't tell whether they hurt because the water is far too hot or far too cold. At any rate I can't stay in the bath, because it hurts too much. I try with my hands to see if the water is too hot or too cold. Of course I find it is warm and not too hot at all. My back, head, shoulders and legs can't stand much either. Clearly the stimuli give me the wrong impression. Luke warm water causes pain in those areas, as if I have burnt myself. When I'm in the bath my knees are right under the tap and if it drips on my knee it feels very painful, and again I can't tell whether it is hot or cold. I have to test it with my hand and of course I find it is cold.

At Scouts I was never able to play in a stream, I couldn't stand the cold water: it was too painful.

When my hair was being washed I used to scream the whole house down. I kept thinking it was burning me as it hurt terribly.

It is a great nuisance while cooking and I easily burn myself. Sometimes I leave my hand in hot water too long, because it takes a while before I realise the water is hot.

When I close my eyes and someone places an ice cube in my hands, it takes some time before I know what it is because I can't feel the cold. I really need to concentrate to be able to feel it.

Eating used to be fraught with difficulties, too. My choice to eat or leave something had little to do with its taste. It was determined by how it felt in my mouth. If something was nice, but felt strange, I wouldn't eat it. The sensation was more important than its taste. I still tend to suck on food and drinks, which is something I used to do to the extreme as a child. Because I still suck on each bite of food, I am a very slow eater. Only recently did I realise that my slowness had another reason. When I was a child, they used to tell me to take small bites. A few days ago at work I wasn't feeling very hungry and I watched other people eating. I noticed how everybody was taking much bigger bites than me. I suddenly realised that I still take small bites as I was taught as a toddler. I did not adjust the size of my bites while growing up; I still eat like a child.

The way food is cut is very important to me. If something is cut in another way than I am accustomed to, I won't eat it. If I order a portion of salami and it has been cut into slices instead of squares, I just can't eat it. I no longer regard it as a portion of salami.

The way in which something is presented on my plate is important, too. If I am served with some food, which I had expected to look different or to be cut or arranged differently, I will refuse to eat it. It isn't a matter of stubbornness, I just can't, it's too difficult and the food no longer resembles its natural appearance.

Art

When I was in primary school I was once ridiculed in art class. We were given some free time and we were allowed to choose what we wanted to draw. I couldn't get down to it. I had been busy all the time arranging my crayons. I arranged them according to colour. I wanted to understand the colours and the differences, but I never could and it frustrated me. I wanted them to remain in a certain order and of course it caused trouble at school. The girl sitting next to me wanted to borrow one of my crayons, but I wouldn't let her because it would destroy the order, which I of course didn't want to happen. She laughed at me, which I thought was cruel.

I was always disappointed after I had made a drawing. I had wanted to see many beautiful colours perfectly merge into each other. I had beautiful images of colours in my mind and they fascinated me. I couldn't forget the colours and colour combinations I had seen elsewhere. I tried to copy them, but I wasn't a good artist, nor did I ever achieve identical colours.

When I used felt-tips I never got round to actually drawing. I used each felt-tip to draw dashes and looked to see which colours would make the best match. I would then put them side by side and would look for the next colour and again and again and again. I would feel very calm and be fascinated by the aspect for a long time, but would I actually get down to drawing? No, all I managed to do was draw dashes, which I enjoyed, and I would only start drawing when others passed comments or began to stare at me. I simply liked drawing dashes with felt-tips, because they were much prettier than drawn with crayons, but I certainly didn't want to *draw* with felt-tips.

Each time I go to the Metropolis cinema I become absorbed in the changing colours of the walls. There are large white walls with special lamps directed on them. The lamps continually change colour with beautiful transitions and many different tones. These colours cover large areas on the walls. They fascinate me and they are so beautiful. I enjoy how they merge into each other! Sometimes it's the colours that attract me more than the film in the cinema. I can look at those colours for hours, and also at colour palettes, which are used to select paints.

However, I hate slide shows. Firstly because slides are usually of poor quality and what you are supposed to see is often missing. In reality everything usually looks quite different because of the light of the lamp in the projector. Slides are very unpredictable;

suddenly you hear their click, which is so unexpected that it hurts my ears. Even if someone warns you that they are going to move onto the next slide, it still hurts. Next you hear the slide moving on and making a grinding noise. Meanwhile the speaker will be giving an explanation, which I can't hear because of the grinding noise, and then suddenly the slide is staring at you. Sometimes it takes longer than other times, because projectors frequently fail. The picture appears, always unexpectedly, and both the moment and the image itself are unpredictable. I often don't know what they are going to show and if I do know in advance, I will not know the colour or the size. I don't know how bright it will be, which makes my eyes hurt. And of course there is the drone of the projector. Such apparatuses are never silent. Most people will think it is a soft noise, but to me it is always quite penetrating.

Noises

My hearing is not right. As a child I was always pleased when we had hearing tests in the medical centre at school. Each time I thought that now they are going to find out what is wrong and they will help me, but none of this happened. My ears were fine. I always wondered how that was possible. I can hear well, but only when everything around me is quiet. If there is the slightest noise in my vicinity, my hearing is no longer perfect. It is as if I can't concentrate on that one particular sound, it is as if they merge into each other, so that I can no longer distinguish between them. They all enter together and there doesn't seem to be any difference between foreground and background noises. They all seem to be just as loud.

At family parties I can't talk to my neighbour because of all the other people talking, the hubbub at a meeting doesn't help at all, and talking in a pub with music on is impossible. I have experienced people breaking off a conversation, because I kept asking them to repeat what they had said. I miss a lot of what is said in conversations. I don't catch it, or only part of it. Because of those incidences, I frequently pretend I have understood, rather than admit how poor my hearing is. Of course others find out, because sometimes my responses are wrong. I have stopped asking people to repeat, because it is impossible and unpleasant. Consequently normal conversations are often out of the question.

Noises make it difficult for me, too. Some noises are painful. The pain limits me enormously and affects my mood. Using a telephone can be made impossible by the small beep you hear each time you press a digit. That beep can be so painful that I will refuse to use the phone. Vacuuming or using a mixer, being in the same room as a washing machine that is on – all these activities are more or less impossible. Even walking down the street and going to a shop can be difficult as it can be painful to me when people suddenly begin to talk. A sharp tone in a voice, but also a whisper can make me flare up or become irritable. Whispering is soft, but can contain several very painful pitches. High pitches trouble me in everything, for example, music, voices and street noise; they occur suddenly and unexpectedly.

My earache caused by noises could be compared with a sudden sharp, excruciating toothache, deep down in the centre of my ear. I often respond by closing my ears without touching them with my hands. I will tense certain muscles around my ears including the masseter. Very often the muscles around my ears are overstretched. The pain travels right across my face and very often I have an inflammation. I regularly visit the kinesthesist. When I have overstretched my masseter I can't even open my mouth. I then have kinesics therapy because of the excruciating pains; I hate those attacks. They are almost unbearable, the pain gives me a temperature and I tend to sleep all day so that I don't feel them as acutely. I have frequently had to ask for sick leave and if I want to get through the day without the pain driving me mad, I need to be able to sleep as a course of prevention. It is only when I sleep that my ears don't hurt. It can be so extreme that I have earache from the moment I get up. I can feel the pain several times a day, which is why I need a lot of sleep. It can be a chronic pain not necessarily triggered by noise. Those are the hardest days. The pain also depends on the weather. High air pressure causes more pain, however it means that when I'm abroad, where there is a different air pressure, it often doesn't bother me at all and painful noises don't bother me as much.

Some noises are frightening even though they don't hurt: the rustling of a plastic bag, a flushing toilet – I panic as soon as I hear these noises. They cause fear rather than pain. It is hard to explain why fear suddenly hits me, and I can't resist it.

I use the radio or my own music to drown out unpleasant sounds. When a certain noise bothers me the best solution may be to put on some music. If I turn the music up enough, I don't hear the other noises and they don't bother me as much. It also helps me relax and recover. However, if the music is really loud I can't stand it. Music in discothèques or certain pubs annoys me, but even gentle music in the background irritates me. I can't stand music that I can hear but isn't loud enough. The music becomes an irritant. I will only put on music if I can turn it up fairly high. I can't stand music in the background. I'd rather not have any music on at all. Sometimes it's not nice for the people around me when I turn up the music, but I can't wear headphones or earplugs because they shut me off from my environment, which isn't acceptable to me either.

I feel that due to my autism I don't hear many things, which is not helped by wearing earplugs or headphones. It is as if I am losing a grip on my surroundings. I can't stand earplugs anyway because they irritate my ears and my voice sounds different. I can't tell whether my tone is too loud or too soft and I can't hear other people speaking to me. I want to know where each sound comes from or what causes it. Sometimes it becomes a real obsession and I lose touch with reality searching for the cause. I am not open to anything else. I guess it may be caused by my sense of having lost my grip. In order to register all the sounds, I lose control of what is happening around me. Sometimes I can't exclude certain sounds, and any slight background noise may claim all my attention, so that I can no longer listen to anything else. I can't concentrate on that one little sound. All the other sounds come in at the same time and it is one big mess – the stream of sounds, all mixed up and indistinguishable. It is like eating vegetable soup, so well blended that you can't recognise any of the vegetables. If someone asks you to indicate when you are putting a carrot in your mouth, while you can't even taste any carrot and you certainly can't see any, it is rather difficult.

I often don't hear someone talking to me. People will ask me if I'm deaf. Of course I'm not deaf, my hearing is very astute, and I can hear sounds nobody else can hear. I often hear sounds very distinctly, where others need to concentrate to be able to hear them. Yet when people address me I usually don't hear, unless they attract my attention. I advise everybody to call my name first before they speak to me; otherwise I am not aware that people are speaking to me. I hear the voice, but don't register the words - – the words don't reach me. There are other sounds – very often in the background – requiring my attention. I am not always aware that people are expecting a response from me. I can hear them and I know what they are saying but I don't realise that they are waiting for me to answer or give a sign of acknowledgement.

When I used the phone at home, I would always retire to an empty room and close the door. My family never understood why. They often used to make remarks about it, but I had no alternative. If my father was turning the pages of the newspaper while I was on the phone, it would make me lose concentration. I could no longer follow the telephone call and the rustling pages of the newspaper would drown the voice at the other end of the line.

As a child, watching television would sometimes be spoilt by somebody speaking during the programme, and I was considered 'unreasonable' or 'very difficult' because I always reacted so vehemently. The two aspects combined were too much for me. I can't handle two noises at the same time. If I want to watch something on television everybody around me needs to be very quiet, otherwise I can't manage.

On the other hand I sometimes think I hear too much, that the sounds are too loud. Noises frighten me and I can't cope. If they are drilling in the house, I will always go outside, I have no choice, and the same applies when a vacuum or a mixer are being used. I might even leave the house when I hear the rustling of a plastic bag, a chair being moved, the rattling of cutlery or the sound of a spoon in a cup. I sometimes cover my ears at apparently ridiculous moments, simply because others begin to laugh.

Music used to be hopeless, too. My brothers liked watching *Top of the Pops* on television and I couldn't stand it. I would refuse to enter the room and they sometimes used loud music to keep me out of the living room or their bedrooms.

I have also noticed that noises cause me to make involuntary movements. If I interrupt a movement, without realising why, it is because I am confused. A particular noise has stopped. It will take some time before I can connect the movement to the noise and for a little while I am quite muddled. I don't realise that because I interrupted a certain movement, it is more difficult to connect a particular movement with a particular noise, but then I will suddenly resume the movement and if I hear the noise again I will realise that I was making the noise myself, which pleases me.

Certain sounds have always fascinated me, even as a child. I loved playing marbles because of the noise they made. The recurring sound of rolling marbles intrigued and calmed me. I felt safe. I preferred to play with them on my own so that I could hear the noise clearly and wouldn't be disturbed.

Even now I love such objects. I can easily entertain myself with scissors for an hour, opening and closing them and listening to the sound they make. I also frequently use my rain stick, it is a fantastic instrument with a lovely clattering noise, slow and fast, loud and soft. It really makes me feel calm and the sound doesn't hurt my ears, because I am making it myself and therefore I am in control. It is a sound that is difficult to describe, which makes it fascinating. Moreover, it is a beautiful stick with painted designs in different colours, with little dots painted close to each other. They create a relief pattern, which I like because running my fingers down the pipe gives a pleasant feeling.

I often play with a tap, I love opening and shutting it in rapid succession. I like listening to the sound of running water and stopping it suddenly. I like moving the tap backwards and forwards while the water is running, watching the stream of water twisting crazily, and I like the sound it makes. A dripping tap is fantastic to listen to.

I went to a lecture in a big hall. The acoustics were excellent; the speaker articulated well and spoke clearly and understandably into the microphone. And yet there was a certain moment when I could no longer pay attention to the lecture. I could no longer concentrate on her voice because there was another noise that was stronger. A few tables behind me someone was slowly clicking his pen. To me this sound was as strong as the sound of the speaker and I couldn't block out the noise. This often happens with sounds, they are all just as loud as each other. Sometimes there doesn't seem to be any difference between background noises and other sounds, as if background noises don't exist. Noises are noises, and everything hits me with the same intensity. It used to bother me during lessons at school. I could no longer pay attention to the teacher, for example, because the strip lights were humming. The humming was far too loud to be able to hear the voice clearly or to be able to distinguish it from the humming. And yet my peers in the classroom hardly heard the humming, or didn't hear it at all.

Feeling

I suffer from a repetitive peculiarity: I jiggle my leg all the time. When my mother asks me to stop it at the breakfast table in the morning, I am irritable and awkward; I feel upset and impotent, and for the next few hours I will be in a bad mood. I feel angry and threatened as my sense of security and confidence has been taken away from me.

If I jiggle at other moments, my boyfriend will jiggle along. He allows me to jiggle and I feel understood. But I'm angry if he doesn't jiggle in the same rhythm, I want him to stop immediately. I want him to do it my way, only in my rhythm. If I am jiggling my leg I can't stop it, even if other people are present.

When I am at home, I really enjoy swinging on a chair. I like swinging my head, as well as biting my fingers or a taut rubber band. I also enjoy rubbing my feet against each other which makes me feel more at ease and really good. I begin to feel relaxed and I miss not being able to do it. I don't do it all the time, and certainly not for hours on end (like jiggling my legs).

I suppose it is like eating chocolate. Some people say it gives you a good feeling because it releases a substance called lecithin, which makes you feel good. The same applies to jiggling. It is as if it releases a substance to my brain, which gives me that sense of wellbeing.

My sense of feeling differs considerably from other people's. For instance, I like rubbing my feet firmly on the carpet or over a mattress, until they begin to glow and feel different. Many times my feet have begun to bleed.

Stepping across a tiled floor is a wonderful experience; I don't raise my feet and don't really step, but slide along rubbing them on the tiles. I enjoy feeling the join between the two tiles. At other times I will step and bang my feet on the floor. I suppose it is more like stomping, but not too hard, just hard enough to give me a slightly painful feeling, which I enjoy. After a while it begins to glow; it's a lovely sensation. Stepping on certain other surfaces can be awkward. I find it difficult to step on carpets or pebbles, and to walk in the woods or in the dunes. An uneven surface is very difficult for me, which also applies to crossing over something. An unexpected step upwards or downwards can be difficult because I can't see how high or deep it is and need to hold on to something. It is as if I can't gauge depths. I always have to hold on when I want to go up or downstairs.

If tiles have different colours, I can't decide which colour to step on. I will begin to worry and can't continue. I can't move, because I can't decide where or on which colour I should place my foot. I try to understand the colours and look for logic, which also applies to tiles with joins, because I can't decide which would be the best spot for the join to touch my foot. Stepping on stones with an obscure design isn't easy either. I will then be fascinated by the designs on the tiles, I lose myself in them and once again I can't move on. I can look at the obscure design for hours trying to make sense of it.

There are some smells I can't stand at all. Usually they don't bother other people and yet they are undesirable to me. My scent is much keener. My nose is very sensitive. On the other hand there are odours that nobody likes, but I love. For instance, I adore sweaty feet, the smell of perspiration and cat pee – delightful aromas, enough to make my day a success!

I have gradually learnt to respond casually to touch, even though it affects me differently. I usually manage, except when people touch me very gently, which I can't stand at all. Touch is fine, but not if it is gentle, at least not on me, I can't bear it.

It is fine if someone grabs me by the arm firmly, it isn't painful, but if someone touches me very softly or rubs my arm or hand, it really hurts. It is unbearable and consequently makes me unmanageable – I will flare up. It's not so much the pain, but the annoying and unpleasant feeling. It is as if I have an inflammation of the skin and the nerves just below. I can't compare it with any other pain. A knock on the head is not as bad, and even a burn or a cut or graze is preferable to a soft stroke.

I can't stand anything wet. If I need to go to the toilet and I would like to wash my hands, then there will be difficulties if the tap is wet, because I won't want to touch it. Nor will I ever dry my hands on a used towel. I just can't bear the feeling of a wet towel. Washing an apple or a tomato isn't easy either, nor opening a door by a wet door handle. I hardly ever touch my car with my bare hands; I will first pull my sleeves over my hands. The same applies to touching metal. I don't like metal, or the feeling of it. It makes me shiver and feel sick. All wet things make me feel that way, but metal is the worst.

I love touching things and I wish I could touch everything. I don't feel I know something until I have been able to touch and feel it. The tactile aspect gives me a lot of information, which I can't acquire in any other way and is very important to me. If I can't touch and feel it, I don't know what something is like. The most important thing about objects is how they feel to me. When I go to a museum I always want to touch everything, but there are a lot of museums where it is not allowed. It frustrates me and ideally I shouldn't go to such a museum. The need to touch, and the frustration when I can't, is so great that it will spoil the visit. I feel like someone who is terribly hungry, who is allowed to smell wonderful food, but not allowed to eat it. The tactile aspect is also important when buying clothes. I often buy clothes because they feel nice and not because I like the colour or the style. Clothes should feel good and yet some items hurt me. The material might feel too coarse or irritate me, which makes it unbearable and impossible to wear. The same applies to food. I like touching my food, particularly if it is something new.

Elastic items are the most preferable to touch: soft items that can be compressed and won't lose shape, or stretching items that can take on different shapes. They give my skin a sensation that I can't explain, but which fascinates and pleases me. Subsequently I like Plasticine, dough and rubber bands; I can play with them for hours. I also have a plastic bag that makes an unpleasant sound, but feels good. It is very soft and can be scrunched into a tight ball. I always have it with me, so that I can touch it from time to time, because it relaxes me.

As a child I always enjoyed someone squeezing me and even now I enjoy heavy pressure on my body. It feels good and makes me feel secure. Similarly I enjoy a hard rub on my back.

Seeing

Sometimes it is difficult for me to visually distinguish between foreground and background. I often perceive incorrectly and can't see what is background and foreground, which explains why I frequently can't recognise objects if I have not been able to look or stare at them for quite some time.

At Scouts there was a flip-chart in front of the green door. The sheets created a large white surface. I only saw a white area on the door and I didn't notice that there was something in front of the door. I wondered how that white area got there; I didn't understand the situation immediately. I really needed to concentrate to see what was in front of the door – to see what was foreground and what was background.

I need plenty of time to observe everything around me. I see so many things that are meaningless to me. I need more time to see what they are. I need time to impose meaning on what I see, and if the time isn't available, it will remain meaningless, confusing and vague. Once there was a packet of cigarettes lying against a teacup. I couldn't make out what it was. The packet was lying against the handle of the cup and the two merged into each other, so that I couldn't recognise the cup or the packet. I thought it was a very strange object, something I had never seen before. At moments like that I will probably stare to try and understand what I see. For example, I once saw a printer merging into the wallpaper, because I couldn't see that the printer was standing against the wall. It looked as if it was hanging from the wall and it looked so strange that I couldn't identify it.

Sometimes it is difficult for me to distinguish individual words, both visually when I see something written down and orally when I hear someone speak. I might attach the latter part of a previous word to the first part of the next word so that the two words look different or sound different and I no longer understand them. It is more likely to happen with people whose voices I'm not used to. It is quite embarrassing and it means I sometimes don't understand people. I just don't hear the pause between words when people are talking. Visually I don't see how letters relate. I can't see which letters belong to each other.

Visually I see things differently. Sometimes I see in fragments. Visual stimuli enter my brain, but it happens so quickly that I can't handle it and the stimuli don't actually reach me. Suddenly there will be an image that has been accepted and I can see the picture. Next I will be taking in apparently meaningless things, followed by a meaningful image, a fragment. It mainly happens in situations where it is difficult for me to have a clear picture of what is happening or when everything happens too quickly. It might happen while I am driving, which is quite frightening.

Movements

I am terrified of things that suddenly move. Birds are a good example. For instance, if they suddenly fly up, it creates so many stimuli, which I haven't been able to prepare myself for, that my eyes hurt and my head aches. I never know where those birds will fly and whether they will return. And if they come back, where are they going to land?

I'm also very afraid of big machines, big buildings and mountains. They are too enormous for me. I can't comprehend what they are and they frighten me. I'm equally afraid of large groups of people. Large masses are beyond me; moreover, they move and are unpredictable. I prefer to stay clear. I'm afraid of the shadows of people, appearing out of the blue and disappearing without further notice. A shadow moves very unpredictably, it can increase in size and decrease, come nearer or move away. Dark bin bags scare me, too, because I can't cope with the enormous impression they make on me. Nor do I like being in wide open spaces, certainly not if there are many people around, such as in market squares, or in quieter areas such as fields. When I'm at the centre of such an open expanse, there are too many things I need to keep an eye on at once. Something could move somewhere unexpectedly and I'm continually trying to prepare myself for such a movement without ever being successful. I don't like waiting on. a bridge either.

Chapter 4

Communication and Language

Communication with people can often be very difficult. The way I use and understand words may not be how they were intended; I treat words differently. I am often told that I take things too literally and I constantly correct people. I always end up having arguments or conflicts and cause misunderstandings because I use words 'differently'. I want a word to be used correctly. It is either right or wrong. I feel people take too many liberties in this respect, and I can't do that, I simply can't.

One day, the plumber was at my house and he needed something to put water in. He asked if I had a small bucket. I said, "No, I haven't, I haven't got any small buckets." He looked at me in surprise and said a larger bucket would do just as well, as long as it could contain water. He pointed to the corner of the room and said he could surely see some buckets there. Of course, I knew there were buckets there, but I was looking for a small one. I did not realise that the main point was that it should simply be able to hold water. He had asked for a small bucket, so I was looking for a small bucket.

I often misinterpret what people are saying. People often have to explain to me what they mean and I will say, "If that is what you mean, you should have said it like that and not confused me." At times like that I cannot be swayed.

If someone tells me that he has been brooding over something all day, or can't concentrate, this is bound to cause an argument because to me that message is not clear at all. I feel that he does not express himself very well, and does not say what he really means. I will keep harping on about it until I know exactly what he means, because otherwise I just don't know, I would not understand his message, it would not reach me. Eventually, after a long argument, it appears that he just wanted to say that he didn't feel well. Then I will keep going on about how he should have said so clearly and how in future he should give no more vague messages. I will insist that he says, "I don't feel well." Only then will I be able to carry on communicating with him. Only then can the conflict stop and I can be calm again. Of course, by that time any real communication has become impossible, as I will have ignored that person's feelings completely. What matters to me at that moment is not the other person or his feelings, but the correct use of words.

Although I know that it isn't right, I just cannot accept such descriptions. He should say what he means. As a result, people sometimes find me a nuisance, especially people who are dear to me. It may seem as if I act like this deliberately, but I simply don't understand if people talk 'differently' and so I really cannot cope with it. I don't want to catch people out on their words, I don't want to be overly literal, but otherwise I don't understand what is being said. Each time something like this happens I get angry with myself and feel that I should have been more flexible. In retrospect I usually recognise that I was wrong, but at the time I cannot fight it. The chaos and confusion are then so great that it makes me feel bewildered. No matter how much I want to change I really can't, and, believe me, I do want to change. In fact, there is nothing I would love more.

Language

I interpret language too literally. For instance, people should never tell me, "That will be nice." I don't understand why people say such things. They can't look into the future, can they? And why say something you cannot be sure about? I don't understand this. Surely there is no point? That is not what words are for.

If someone asks me, "When is the library open?" I will become awkward and often this will lead to trouble. What kind of question is this? I do understand, "What are the library's opening hours?" Or, "What day is the library open?" These are questions I can answer. But the first question makes me feel utterly powerless; I cannot deal with it.

I used to keep repeating my question until I received a satisfactory response. If I asked, "When are we going for a walk?" and I got an incorrect answer, I'd keep repeating the question over and over again. I'd repeat the question because I hadn't had an answer yet. But the other people would also keep repeating the same reply. Wasn't it obvious that I'd like a different answer? I was told we'd go for a walk tomorrow afternoon, but I wanted to know at what time.

My coping skills used to be limited, so I was unable to explain in a different way that I had not yet had an answer to my question. Of course, everyone thought I was playing games and people became angry, while I felt totally misunderstood. I was longing for an answer, but people didn't understand me and that made me feel miserable.

One day I was going to a barbecue. I was wearing short sleeves and my watch was clearly visible. Suddenly, a friend asked, "Dominique, what time is it?" I knew he could see my watch and therefore he ought to know that I knew the time. So I thought he wanted to know if I knew without looking at my watch. I thought about this for a second and said, "Possibly eight thirty or perhaps only seven o'clock." "No," I continued, "I'm sorry, I can't tell you." And I carried on eating without looking up. The guy was staring at me goggle-eyed. When I saw the look in his eyes I asked why he was staring at me like that and if he really wanted to know what time it was. He did. I looked at my watch, told him the time and to me that was the end of the matter. I only wondered why he had asked such a vague question.

Here's another example: during a Tai Ji lesson the instructor was talking to us while she showed us what to do. She told a story and we had to imagine the situation and do what she described. At one point we were a cat rolling on our backs, stretching ourselves and then rolling around again. Then the cat lay on its back again, in the sun. It was enjoying the sun shining on its bare tummy. When she said, "bare tummy" I immediately grabbed my T-shirt and wanted to pull it up so that my belly would show. After all, we had to act out what was being said. Fortunately, the person next to me stopped me just in time and explained that we didn't have to act out this bit literally. That was very hard for me. We had to act out everything she said, but some things we were not allowed to act out? One thing was allowed but another one was not? How could we tell the difference? I couldn't understand it at all.

And here's another example: I was going to see a show with some friends. We had arranged that one of us would order tickets and we'd agreed on a price category. One week later I saw the friend who was going to order them. He came up to me and told me that the tickets were 1150 Belgian francs per person, so it would be 2300 Belgian francs for my boyfriend and me. Straight away I said, "Wow, that's great!" Apart from that I did not react and just carried on with what I was doing. Of course, he didn't only want to tell me the price of the tickets he also wanted me to pay for them, but I didn't realise. I thought it was simply a comment, not a demand for money. When I later told my boyfriend, it suddenly dawned on me and I was very embarrassed.

This kind of incident happens all the time. When my boyfriend says, "Dominique, please get me a bottle of Coke from the crate on the balcony", this may give rise to unanticipated difficulties. If I go to the balcony and the crate is empty but there is a bottle next to the crate, I will not bring back a bottle of Coke. If I am asked to bring back a bottle of Coke from the crate, then I will only bring back Coke from the crate. After all, that is what I was asked to do. I fail to see that bringing back the Coke is what really matters! I am oblivious to it. The essence of the assignment is not clear to me. I get fixated on the tangible, the literal aspect. It doesn't occur to me that this is wrong even if I return and say, "I haven't got any Coke left. The crate was empty; there was only a bottle nearby." It's only when my boyfriend then looks at me in a funny way that I understand.

Expressions

I often don't understand expressions. The images disturb me. When I hear an expression I visualise it literally and I find it difficult to distance myself from this literal-mindedness. The real sense of the expression is too distant, too abstract and I don't understand. I don't see any connection with the actual meaning.

I was aware of this from an early age. So when we were taught about expressions at primary school I was very pleased, because now their meaning and origin would be explained. We had a closer look at how they originated. I sensed that I was sadly lacking in this area and really wanted to be taught about it so I could try to catch up. Even now expressions fascinate me, although it always makes me very nervous whenever any new ones are used, as I am unable to grasp their meaning. They are so confusing that I become awkward.

The literal-mindedness with which I interpret everything also causes other difficulties. This is because I tend to believe everything that people say, even totally absurd things or things that are just not possible. At first I keep falling for it. Often I quickly realise that it is impossible or that I should have known that it wasn't true. Yet I keep failing to realise this any sooner. I lack the insight to get the message quicker and to react more appropriately.

This frequently makes me come across as very naïve. I don't understand why people sometimes say things that aren't true.

Something like it happened recently. Several times I have been to the Nekkerspoel district in Mechelen and I recognise the buildings whenever we drive past. One day I was a passenger in my boyfriend's car. When driving past the canal in Mechelen we saw a boat with a sign displaying in huge letters, 'The Nekkerspoel'. My boyfriend said to me, "Look, here is the Nekkerspoel." That wasn't true, of course, but I still believed him. At the same time I knew perfectly well that the Nekkerspoel wasn't there at all. So I thought that you could walk all the way to the Nekkerspoel behind the sign. I then reasoned that this wasn't possible either, because I saw a sign saying the Nekkerspoel was ten kilometres away. So what my boyfriend had told me wasn't true. For the rest of that car journey I kept wondering why my boyfriend had said that. I felt hurt and terribly rejected.

Some people take advantage of this and spin me one story after another. They seem to take great pleasure in it. At times like that I sometimes feel like a seaside amusement. People tell me something, I believe them and then they laugh at me. Sometimes they never stop. Even my parents and my brothers do it.

One day at secondary school, we had fish fingers. At home everyone told me they consisted of a special type of fish with fingers instead of fins. Of course, I believed them. Every evening after I came home from school my first question would be, "What's for dinner?" Whenever it was fish fingers, my mum answered, "Fingers" and I thought of fish swimming around with fingers instead of fins. It wasn't until the age of twenty-two that I discovered fish with fingers did not exist. That was when they really started to mock me. There are dozens of examples like this – sometimes big, sometimes only small ones.

For instance, I recently went to a quiz, together with a few Scout members, my brother and my boyfriend. My boyfriend answered all the questions on geography, which is his strong point. There was a question about a village with the River Seine running through. My boyfriend asked me to check the course of the River Seine with my brother. My brother said, "Through Brussels." Although this was obviously a joke, I simply passed on his answer. Of course, our whole table was in stitches.

On another occasion I was at a Scouts party when a leader came up to me and said that they had invented a new road sign – 'end of roundabout'. Although this was clearly a joke, I didn't think it was funny. I didn't get the joke. I kept thinking about a suitable location for such a sign. Not on the roundabout itself, of course, because that has no end. So then I thought it should be positioned at the start of each street that came off the roundabout. But I thought that this would be a bit silly because they would have to use many road signs, which would be a very large investment for something that wasn't really necessary.

A few Scouts started to laugh at me. Other people were annoyed because my reaction to a joke was so odd. It must have come across as if I wanted to ruin the atmosphere, as if I begrudged them a good joke. When I realised it was a joke, I still failed to see what was so funny about it. I couldn't understand why someone would laugh at it. I tried to get it, but couldn't.

During an open day at the school of one of the Scout leaders I went to look at his completed project. To activate the project you had to push a button once. I was looking at it for half an hour and knew fairly well how it worked by then. Then the lad said I should press the button. I did but he said I had to do it again. I said that surely once was enough. He said that he could get it to work by pressing the button once but that I apparently could not and that I really had to press again. The mechanism – strangely enough – didn't seem to work with me, although it did with everyone else. I pressed again. By then the machine was already working very hard. He said I had to press once more and keep the button pressed and then press again because the machine wasn't working properly. Of course the machine was working properly and I could see that, but still he maintained that it wasn't working properly, so it had to be true. Otherwise he wouldn't have said it. I kept on pressing the button for five minutes.

Afterwards he told me he had tricked me. Of course it wasn't true that the machine was broken. I could see that for myself. But then why had he said that I needed to press the button over and over again? I just believed him and so was ridiculed again.

Here's another example: I was in a car with a friend and I told him my cat was sad because my hamster had died and the cat saw me putting it in the dustbin. The friend asked if I was quite sure the hamster was dead. I said that it felt cold and therefore had to be dead. The friend said that hamsters could also feel cold to the touch when they hibernate. He said that the animal would probably have been asleep. I knew full well that the hamster was not hibernating yet he said it might be sleeping. I believed him and felt guilty.

Some months later this incident came up in conversation. The friend discovered I had believed him the first time. He immediately confessed it had been a joke and that he thought I would have realised. I felt miserable. How could I have been so stupid! How could I have believed all that nonsense even though I knew perfectly well that this hamster didn't hibernate! It was a very painful moment.

I then reflected on how many similar incidents I experience every day or every week. The embarrassing fact was that this particular one had come up in conversation. Who knows how many things I believe that aren't true and that I don't find out about? It makes me feel very sad because I don't understand anything about this complicated world. It happens all the time, usually without me realising it. Knowing that it will keep on happening time and time again without being able to do anything about it is not easy. I know that I will fall for it again tomorrow and again the day after, time and time again.

Imagination and humour

Everything has to be very concrete to me or else I can't cope with it; I don't get it or understand it. An acquaintance of mine had had problems with her neighbours for some time. They are often noisy and cause quite a bit of nuisance in their street. Someone who was following the conversation said that she should mention it to the residents' association. They help with all kinds of things and you could approach them with various complaints. Then the acquaintance with the difficult neighbours mentioned they now had a dog that they couldn't control. The dog would bark for hours on end – even at night. The person who had suggested the residents' association said you could also tell them about it and they would certainly listen. I immediately disagreed with him, because I just could not believe it – not every dog listens when you tell it to be quiet! I kept focusing on the tangible, on the dog. I thought he was going to talk to the dog, not to the residents' association.

I hate imagination; I simply cannot cope with it. Flights of fancy make me feel angry and I can't stand it when someone gives his imagination free rein while I have to listen to it. That provokes an angry reaction in me. As a child I could never take part in pretend games. With the Scouts, especially, this was a downright disaster. I was dragged into them before I knew what was happening. I didn't understand what was going on around me or what others were doing and I couldn't join in.

I also find it hard to cope with humour. Ordinary humour is fine, and I actually really like it. But any humour involving words with a double meaning is too difficult for me. Puns cannot make me laugh.

Sometimes people use humour to lighten a situation that might be difficult. That is another thing I cannot understand. Why do people laugh when they are having a rough time? Why do people start cracking jokes when I have just told them I am in a difficult situation? I certainly can't laugh about it myself.

One night I went to a show in a group of four – all of them close friends. In the car the driver said we were sure to be late. The show started at eight, it was only seven at the time and we were only ten minutes away from our destination. Somehow I knew that it was highly unlikely that we would be late. Yet he said we'd definitely be late. I didn't understand why and was annoyed about it, because I didn't want to be late. Our driver said irritably that we wouldn't be late. I didn't understand why he had said we would.

While we were waiting for the show to begin, I looked at the programme and read that the band was the moral winners of the preselection rounds for the Eurovision song contest. I asked a friend if he knew that. He began to laugh. I said that it must be nice to be the moral winners. This made him laugh even more. I asked him what the matter was. He said that everyone was the moral winner. I didn't understand it at all. In my vocabulary there can only be one winner, as I told my friend. After the concert he explained the concept of a moral winner and that you don't always need to be the best to win. Being a winner sometimes means that you profit from something. Then I understood, but I didn't understand why my friend had been so awkward towards me. Why didn't he simply explain it to me?

There is something that I absolutely detest about myself. Sometimes I don't see people as people but as part of my structure. This mainly happens when I am having a tough time. Fortunately, it doesn't happen very often. At times like that I ignore the person; I can't empathise with them. There are times when I find it hard to imagine they have feelings as to me people are sometimes things or objects. It makes me very angry when I can't mould them; I often have temper tantrums. I want someone to do or say a certain thing at a certain time and nothing else. Of course, people rarely do exactly what I want them to do.

For instance, if something bothers me someone has to ask me, "What is the matter?" They should not ask me anything else. That is just the way it is with me. I won't allow them to be more tactful – to me that is beating about the bush. It makes me angry if they are tactful and I will then not respond, not even if they keep asking me questions or insist. Afterwards I criticise them for not asking me what was bothering me and for not worrying about me. They feel that they did make the effort, show their sympathy and demonstrated they were there for me. But I didn't notice. After all, you only show sympathy if you do it my way.

If someone says something, I often repeat it. When I was a child everyone thought I was annoying and I would regularly be asked to stop playing games. Games? I didn't know what they were talking about. I wasn't playing, was I? I was just sitting on my chair at the table. So what was the game they wanted me to stop playing?

Luckily, I soon realised that repeating everything was not appreciated and not normal. So I tried to control it, but that was hard. Even now I sometimes repeat whole conversations to myself. I used to do this especially during lessons. I am sure the words would have sunk in without me having to repeat them.

Chapter 5

Learning and Linking

I feel as if I'm living in a different world and as if I think differently. I feel as if all behaviours have to be acquired. If I haven't learnt something, then I can't do it. I can't put things that have never been explained to me into practice.

Let me give an example. During a meeting at my house I had to phone someone whose name and address I had. I said I couldn't phone him because I didn't have his number. Someone told me that his number was in the phone book. I replied that although I knew that, I didn't have the number and so couldn't phone him. The other person again said I could look it up in the phone book, which I then did. I have learnt to do this and have been able to fall back on that skill ever since.

The link was made. The behaviour has been learnt and from then on I can always put it into practice. If I hadn't been told that time, I would still be unable to do it now. I am not flexible enough to gain that insight myself. Although I do know the purpose of a phone book and how to use it, I don't make the link.

A head full of pegs

I will always put into practice what I have been taught, but I cannot adapt it easily to a changing situation. If I learnt it in a particular situation, then I will always be able to use it in that situation. But if anything changes about the situation then it becomes very difficult and I will often not be able to cope. The link with the original situation is completely missing, I can then see no connection at all between the two and so I can't act appropriately.

It's as if my head is full of pegs. Each peg has a name and there are small items hanging from each peg. If I need to do something, I look at a peg to see how it should be done. If it is on the peg then I will take it and use it. If it is not on the peg, well, bad luck. It will then have to be added first. Sometimes I am like a computer: what isn't there can't come out. Sometimes that can be pretty annoying because acquired habits apply in certain situations but have to be adapted in other circumstances, which is something I can't do. In some cases I can do something, yet not in other ones. I lack the insight. As a result my behaviour is often maladjusted. I can't re-examine situations taking new facts into consideration. I cannot judge them myself.

For instance, I always get up in plenty of time to take a bath. I have learnt that getting up late means no bath. If I wake up three minutes late, I will therefore not have a bath. In retrospect this seems ridiculous, it was only three minutes and besides, I had plenty of time, as I had nothing else to do that morning. But nevertheless I was unable to review the situation. I stick to what I have learnt. I lack flexibility.

The peg system is sometimes very annoying and sometimes dangerous, for instance when learning to drive. I managed to do this after a long time by taking lots of extra lessons and changing the instruction module. I was told to brake when you see someone suddenly crossing the road, avoid cyclists, slow down when you see an obstruction... so that's what I did. But I wasn't told to slow down in narrow streets with oncoming traffic. Consequently, I kept accelerating and pulled the most dangerous stunts.

The other day I was driving on a major road with my boyfriend. Someone speeded onto our road from the right. "Swerve!" my boyfriend shouted. I couldn't do it, because what the other car did was not allowed, it was wrong and I always stand by that. I am simply unable to judge the situation for myself or to adapt my driving to new circumstances. Since this incident, that situation has now also been pegged and in future I will be able to apply that rule. At times when it becomes nearly fatal I am able to enter it into the computer myself. I am then incredibly proud that I have added it myself, but at the same time I feel apprehensive as there will be many other dangerous things that I am doing wrong.

Essentials and trivia

Some things are impossible for me because I have learnt them differently. One day around dinnertime I went to the pub with my boyfriend. We were hungry and wanted a bite to eat. I really fancied pancakes, so I ordered them. However, I couldn't eat them. I have learnt that pancakes are not a proper meal and that you do not eat sweet things as your evening meal. I really fancied them, but still felt obliged to leave them.

If I need to learn something new, it takes me a great effort to concentrate. Learning anything is much slower for me and takes a lot more time. Doing things also takes longer, demands more attention and requires a much greater effort. Sometimes it seems as if I'm not paying any attention when in fact I am.

The problem is just that I cannot distinguish between essentials and trivia. When the teacher at school explained something but at the same time made a comment about a window that was open, then for the next ten minutes I would invariably be wondering if the rules she was explaining would also apply if the window wasn't open. But of course I could not explain that this was going on in my head, and so for the next ten minutes she would find it 'difficult to focus my attention on the lesson'. And yet I was paying close attention to the subject!

What's more, I can do only one thing at a time. If I need to do two things at the same time, then I'll first have to work out how to split them up. I have to do that correctly before I can start. Of course, other people have made much more progress by then. Once I've done one thing and started on the next I have to make sure I don't lose track of the first one in my head. Remembering things is not so easy either because I need to make the right connections otherwise I can't retrieve them.

I feel as if I need to remember things almost manually. This is why I believe I was never able to understand maths. Reading comprehension was beyond me as well, in fact, it still is. When I've seen a film or read a book or even a comic I am unable to repeat the story immediately afterwards. Problems occur even while I am still reading; I have to keep going back in a book. I can't read a book without making notes. When I've heard or read a fairytale I have to ask the children to remind me how the prince turned into a king.

Sometimes I make the wrong connections. I have just moved house and have got new cups: yellow, green and blue ones. I never drink coffee. Yet on the day of the move I had some coffee from a yellow cup. Now I can't drink tea from that cup anymore, because ever since that time the yellow cup has been meant for coffee. Sometimes I resist and still want to drink tea from the yellow cup. But I can't do it. I always end up having to pour away the tea. The yellow cup has been programmed as a coffee cup.

At work I am obliged to drink milk that comes in blue cartons. I went to the shop to buy milk but all the blue cartons had gone. There were still some red cartons of the same brand but that wouldn't do for me. I then decided not to buy any milk and also prepared a different meal that night.

In fact, for many products it is a downright disaster if there are different brands. I quite understand that this is silly but I can't help it, I just feel a great resistance at times like that.

Some time after the incident I've just described I really wanted to have some milk, so I did buy the red carton. But the milk went sour in the fridge because I couldn't bring myself to drink milk from a red carton.

A similar thing happened when I needed some vinegar recently. It was quite a problem to find it because I happened to be in a store where I'd never bought vinegar before, so I didn't know where to find it. Also, at home we used to have one particular brand of vinegar, with a blue label. Of course, I couldn't find that brand on the shelves. I did find a different bottle of vinegar with a blue label. I tried to force myself to buy that bottle but couldn't. I couldn't believe it was vinegar, although it said so on the bottle. I was convinced that this vinegar was different from 'ordinary' vinegar. I had to have 'real' vinegar, so I left the bottle on the shelf. I went to a small grocer where they did have our usual brand.

It is very annoying that I don't understand certain things or can't make the right connections. At a family party my youngest brother said he was going to treat the wooden floor in the bedroom. We asked him what he intended to do with the walls. He had wallpaper with an island pattern, but he might paint the walls instead as he also liked plain walls. My oldest brother said that wallpaper could also be washed; my youngest brother thought that was a good idea. I was amazed at the amount of work he was planning to do. He told me it would take a few hours but I thought it was bound to take much longer. After all, I kept holding on to the idea of a plain wall. I thought he wanted to wash the wallpaper until it became plain.

During preparations for a Scout camp we dropped off some material in a Scout leader's garden. He keeps chickens in his garden. I asked him if he had lots of eggs. That wasn't the case. The chickens were too old to lay many eggs. They did lay some but only a few. I asked him if he couldn't let some of them hatch so he would get young chickens again. He said he couldn't because he didn't have a cockerel to sit on them. I was amazed and said I didn't know a cockerel had to sit on the eggs. The others of course thought this was hilarious.

Chapter 6

Planning and Structure

Many of my problems can be sidestepped by preplanning. Schedules are very important to me. I need to know well in advance what is going to happen, how, who is involved and so on. Everything is always planned. When my boyfriend comes over for a day or even for a couple of hours our first task is always to draw up a schedule. In fact, I would even prefer to do this beforehand. I cannot function without planning. Any change of plan leads to frustration, powerlessness, anger and anxiety. People must come and go according to plan. Being late causes difficulties, but so does being early, and people who leave earlier or later than planned also make me feel uncomfortable.

Schedules

One day a friend dropped by. We had made a plan. I was first going to buy fruit in the village and later I was going to buy vinegar and kitchen foil with her in the next town because they don't stock those products in the small village shop. That was our plan. I went to the shop, bought fruit and also saw kitchen foil and vinegar, but didn't buy them since we would be buying those in town that afternoon. When I came home my friend asked if I had got everything. I told her about the kitchen foil and the vinegar. She couldn't understand why I hadn't bought those items and thought it was silly of me. Yet I couldn't help it because that was what we had planned. And so we drove the ten kilometres and back for something I could just as easily have bought in the village. My friend did her best to persuade me to go back to the village shop but that was impossible to me. I was adamant that we had to drive those ten kilometres. This is incomprehensible to other people, but normal, daily practice to me.

Here's another example: the other day I went to the cinema with my boyfriend. When we were in the car driving home we couldn't get away. The car's ignition was malfunctioning and I couldn't turn my key, so couldn't start the engine. We were there for half an hour. I was beside myself. My boyfriend suggested that we call the breakdown service or go home on the bus. To me this was completely out of the question, even after an hour. I was adamant that we had to go back by car, because we had come by car. Clearly, the plan was to return in the car and so that's the way it should be. Calling the breakdown service was not according to plan, so that wasn't allowed to happen. The fact that the car had broken down didn't change anything. This is the way it should be and not any other way. My boyfriend's suggestions made me feel very angry. I wanted to stay in that car, even if that meant staying till the following morning. I would then adjust my plans and allow for calling the breakdown service the next day, but for now that wasn't an option anymore so I stayed put. Fortunately, I got the ignition to work again after an hour.

Another example is: one night I went out with my boyfriend and parked the car on the quays of the River Scheldt. As usual, we drew up a plan for the evening – we were going to eat chips that night. After we'd stood on the quays for a while we went into town. We arrived at a chip shop where we sometimes stop for a bite, but my boyfriend walked on. I was really upset. We were going to eat chips in town, weren't we? I thought we'd do that immediately and go straight to our destination. Of course, that was silly and we could go for a walk first. I tried to pretend everything was fine. I managed to keep it up for five minutes. After that I could no longer contain myself and we had to plan at what time we'd be having chips, as this was too unclear for me. Then it became a mess, as we hadn't decided on a chip shop. My boyfriend thought it didn't matter where we would eat and, although I realised that it should not matter, I felt totally stuck and awful. I would love to be as flexible as everyone else.

I even plan my sessions with the psychiatrist in advance. I write everything that I want to discuss on a card. If my psychiatrist brings up a different subject that is just bad luck, it simply isn't discussable, not even if it's something insignificant that I find easy to discuss. I will simply not talk about it. It's as if my head won't give me permission to talk about it. Anything unplanned feels bad and I can therefore not bring myself to let it happen. Sometimes that can be annoying, because when I leave the room I curse myself for not responding as I had plenty to say about it, or because it was important or because I just wanted to talk about it. But when my head refuses permission because it hasn't been planned, then it's impossible. Yet if the psychiatrist asks me to put it on the card for next time, I can talk about it easily. If I haven't brought my card along, I'll clam up.

If something has been planned, then it must also take place. I cannot stand changes; I won't tolerate them. If we plan to go to the cinema, then the cinema is where we must go. If that isn't possible for some reason – even a good reason such as a car breaking down – I can't accept it. Although I can appreciate that the cinema may be out of the question, I still can't tolerate any other activity. After all, I won't be able to prepare at such short notice. A different activity doesn't feel right so I won't accept it. I'll then be upset and very angry for the rest of the day.

Once my boyfriend and I were about to leave. We were going to his house to check if there were any emails for me, which is very important to me. We were halfway down the stairs when my boyfriend said he'd left something upstairs. He asked if he could go back up again. It is one of my rules that this must never happen and I already felt quite powerless that it had to happen anyway. Upstairs we couldn't find the piece of paper he was looking for. We were searching for half an hour but couldn't find it. "Now what?" I asked with dismay. "Then we'll just go without it," my boyfriend said, and wanted to leave. But that was out of the question to me. Going upstairs specifically to get something and then going back down without having found it goes against my grain. I was panicking because now we couldn't write any emails, as we couldn't leave. First we had to find the piece of paper and then we'd write emails. This thought had immediately imprinted itself on my mind, which meant that I could not deviate from it. To me that is obvious. I will not skip that step, and that's why I can become frantic if a simple piece of paper can't be found. I really couldn't go on without the piece of paper and because of that the rest of the planning would have to be changed, which made the situation completely unbearable. I was very awkward and aggressive. It felt to me as if things were out of hand; I had got myself into a mess. My boyfriend had to deal firmly with me to calm me down. He has to give me clear, resolute instructions and stick to his guns.

Incidents like these happen quite frequently and are perplexing to other people. If I have planned to go to a party wearing a particular pair of shoes and I can't find them, I am frantic. My whole day stops and I can't go to the party.

Lists

I use lists a lot. I constantly draw up lists and schedules. For instance, I can't go to the shops without a list. Recently, we had an orienteering event with the Scouts and we had to take food along; I was going to bring a tuna salad. I made a list for what I needed and went to the supermarket. When I went to the till with my shopping I passed the mayonnaise. I knew we'd run out of mayonnaise and that I needed it for the tuna salad. Yet I couldn't buy any because it wasn't on my list. I knew I didn't have much time and really needed mayonnaise but still had to leave it on the shelf. I dropped off all my shopping at home and went back to the supermarket with a new list to buy mayonnaise.

Everything I do happens in a specific place. Every activity has its own spot, even at home. If I don't stick to it I become upset. Giving everything its regular place creates the feeling of safety and structure that I so desperately need. If that changes, the feeling of safety and predictability immediately disappears. I hang on to that because I know I will have difficulties otherwise. The trouble doesn't start at the time but usually after the event. For instance, I feel that I need to eat at the table and whenever I eat in front of the TV or on the sofa I get worked up. Things are then no longer clear to me and it's inevitable that one day I won't allow myself to eat at all because eating has lost its regular place. That means that in my mind there is no place left that is suitable for eating. I can't eat at the table anymore because the feeling of resistance is too great; I can't eat on the sofa either because that also triggers resistance. These problems are very hard to solve and make me feel awful and utterly desperate. If this happens with several things at the same time, my life becomes almost intolerable.

For many things I have a set pattern that I follow rigidly. If the pattern is broken life suddenly becomes very difficult. It's almost as if I can hardly remember how to do simple things. If I'm having a wash and I'm interrupted by the telephone I find it very hard to carry on. It also depends a lot on the situation. In a different setting it seems nothing is self-evident anymore. I clearly notice that on holiday, when I am out of my daily wash routine. It is almost as if I have forgotten the order in which I do these things at home. At home I don't forget anything because of the set pattern, but in a different setting this requires a lot of thought.

If I have done something in a certain way a few times, then I need to carry on doing it in the same way. There is no room for change. This makes it easy for me to develop rituals. Sometimes I involve others in this. If something needs to be done at my house and my boyfriend wants to do it to help me, he has to do it exactly according to my pattern. Of course, the pleasure of helping someone soon evaporates. I give detailed instructions on what he has to do, often in a very roundabout way. In my eyes he does everything wrong which often leads to conflicts. After all, trying to follow my pattern exactly is not easy.

To me even stupid things have a set pattern of their own. M&Ms should be eaten in a particular order: one particular colour follows another and not any other way. The segments of an orange should be eaten from small to big. I can sometimes spend fifteen minutes establishing the order, because it needs to be exact.

Often it's the small things that make me face the fact that although I live independently I can't really cope with it. Some small things cause me so much pain that they become big, genuine problems.

One day I was planning to prepare a particular dish. I had planned it that morning. Yet around dinnertime I fancied pasta. Sadly, that wasn't possible because it wasn't planned. But I didn't fancy the other dish either. Because I had been so preoccupied with it that was now no longer good enough. I panicked because I didn't know what to do about the evening meal. So I rang my boyfriend and said, "Tell me to eat pasta for dinner tonight." My boyfriend obliged. He only has to repeat it several times and everything falls into place again. I find this terrible, because at times like that I am using my boyfriend. At times like that someone has to take decisions for me and do it in a very firm manner. I myself tend to present my decision in the form of a question in my overwhelming desire for clarity. I can repeat my question at least a dozen times or ask at least a dozen times what's going to happen now. I do this because I want to be absolutely certain about it. I try to make the other person hesitate. But if they change their mind and suggest something different, then I really start to panic. Only once the planned course of action has been executed do I regain some flexibility.

I frequently ring my boyfriend to ask him for solutions. Recently my car had broken down. When I drove home at three in the morning I noticed that something was wrong. The following day was going to be fairly busy and I didn't know how to include the garage in my planning. So at three thirty in the morning I frantically rang my boyfriend to ask him how to amend my plans.

Leisure time

I am anything but flexible; without a set pattern I have never really felt that I could cope.

I am hopeless at dealing with my time off. I always have to keep busy or else I feel lost and overwhelmed with a sense of powerlessness and despair. Often I just begin to cry out of sheer misery. Well-defined activities suit me best, for instance watching a film is ideal. After all, a film has a clear ending at a certain time. It is not as short as a TV programme (in which case I will soon need to find a different activity) and when it ends it really is all over. Having nothing to do is a nightmare for me. I would rather spend hours sitting in the waiting room at the doctors.

Periods with spare time at hand are always difficult for me. I can't deal with inactivity and not having anything to do. I try to fill every free moment of my time, because otherwise I don't know how to behave. I can't be idle; I always need to keep busy. That is why I often race ahead of myself. I cram my day with activities and even keep myself busy in the odd hour when I'm at home. Quite often I long for rest and I would love to do just nothing for a while. But whenever I do get the chance I still manage to fill my time with plans. I look forward to a day off so I can do whatever I like yet that day never comes, because whenever I am free I feel an even greater need for planning. The result is that I have no time at all.

I function better at times when my diary is fully booked and I have plenty to do. I need to plan everything on paper. This may seem silly but I can't even do the dishes if it is not on my list or in my plan for that day. Only once I have written something down will it be accepted and approved. At the same time recording everything gives me a useful overview. I tend to get lost in the profusion of things if I don't organise everything on paper. I can only get an overview of a situation, a day or a moment if I have written it down and can comprehend it in that way.

All my life people have told me that I can be lazy. I am not – if I don't do something it's because it's not possible and it doesn't fit into my structure.

If someone tells me, "Dominique, go to the shop and buy some butter!" I will often react strongly with, "NO", even if I haven't got anything to do at the time. I just can't do it at the drop of a hat. I need time. With me everything should be announced in advance. So I am not selfish or lazy, I enjoy going shopping for other people. But I would like to be asked at least fifteen minutes beforehand, even if I am twiddling my thumbs at the time. Then I can slot it into my system and make the transition to another activity. I simply can't handle any changes that are too sudden.

Recently the Scouts asked me to pay money into the account of our young people's pub. That morning, as always, I had made a plan. I was going to the bank because I needed to make a few deposits. The request for the pub deposit came much later that day. When I had almost reached the bank I realised that I would also have to make the deposit for the pub. I had brought the money with me in an envelope; I had the account number so everything was fine. Nonetheless I was too petrified to carry out the transaction, as it wasn't planned, and so I did not make that deposit. When I met the lad from the young people's pub that night he was in a bad mood and kept nagging me because I still hadn't done it. The following day I therefore went back to the bank just to make that one deposit. Things like this happen all the time in my life; when I was a child they used to happen frequently. Now I try to prevent it, although my attempts regularly fail. Consequently, I have often been labelled lazy. To me that isn't right, but I can't explain it to anyone because then I have to explain that I am 'different' and I don't want to do that. In fact, I always try to hide it, and that's why it usually ends in a kind of yes-no game. Usually I have to say that I am lazy, because people who don't know me, and that is nearly everyone, must surely think so.

Presents

I can't handle surprises. Nobody is allowed to surprise me, and my boyfriend thinks that's a shame. He always needs to announce in advance where we are going, what we are going to do, how many people will be there, who we are going to see... He surprised me only once. It made me feel so upset and angry that we agreed never to do anything unexpectedly again.

If I have arranged to meet someone, I will go and meet them as planned. Sometimes I happen to be at home – often I will be doing nothing or feel bored – and suddenly someone comes round to suggest doing something together. That is simply impossible. I am just not flexible enough for that. I need more time to prepare, even if I am bored or am not doing anything. People should really not even drop in on me. I have to know the exact day and the exact time in advance. Ideally I also like to know the time they are planning to leave. Of course, that is rather unpleasant. If someone visits me I will immediately ask what time he is planning to leave. I don't mind what time that will be. I don't ask because I hate having company. I only need to know because it is a way to get the situation more under control. Everything needs to be clearly defined. If someone rings the doorbell without an appointment I will not answer the door. That's just not possible; it's too difficult, unexpected and threatening. I will even leave my parents and my brothers standing outside if they arrive unexpectedly. The same goes for my best friends. I cannot handle it.

That's also why I hate unexpected presents. The annoying thing about presents is that I don't know what's inside and so I don't know how I should react. I don't know how to react spontaneously; my reactions have to be well reasoned.

I need so many set patterns because I don't automatically understand things. I have no natural patterns or other patterns to hold on to. This was very obvious when I was a student. What is the main issue and what are the details? No idea! In our year there were eighty students. Yet my course was easy to pick out. It was totally different. It didn't even resemble any of the other ones, the seventy-nine other courses!

Chapter 7

Social Contacts

I am very sociable but only when I feel comfortable and at ease. I have no difficulty with the Scouts, family and friends, but as soon as I am in a different environment I'm at a complete loss. The contrast is enormous. I get very upset and then I can't even maintain a five minute conversation. I can't hold my own during loose contacts. All my social behaviours have been learnt, as I lack such insights myself. I have come a long way in this respect. What comes naturally to anyone else I need to capture intellectually and learn by heart. What anyone else feels intuitively I have to translate into rules, the way you try to understand maths. This is how I managed to survive as a child, even though I couldn't mix easily.

Educational Science Course

The breakthrough came when I did a course in Educational Science at the technical college, where social rules were discussed in great detail. Without the course I would never have become the person I am today and I would be far less sociable. I feel very fortunate that I decided to do the Educational Science course, because I learnt a great deal about feelings there. I just couldn't cope with feelings before. I developed techniques for dealing with feelings, for talking, for taking part in meetings... You could call it a very extensive social skills training. That was just what I needed (and perhaps still need). In order to deal with other people's feelings I need to put on my 'professional hat', otherwise I won't manage. I have to use certain techniques for that.

If I hadn't studied Educational Science I would still be the way I was at sixth form college, which was pitiful. Educational Science was my salvation, my chance of survival. Everything was explained to me. All feelings were discussed, including how to deal with them, where they come from and how they can change. I have learnt them all in a purely technical way.

I also put into practice exactly what they told me on the course. In my behaviour I copy what it says in the books. I was unable to discover all those rules of behaviour by myself. In my profession as a care worker I put the theory rigorously into practice. I have to go by the book because if I don't I will have to interpret the social situation myself, which is hard for me. If I don't go by the book I am lost. That is what makes loose contacts so tricky; these are not described in any of the books.

I can cope better as a leader because then I'm in charge. It's easier, because I am the one who decides everything.

I also did extensive assertiveness training. I had no idea how to ask for something in a shop properly or how to make a complaint; I just didn't have a clue. But once it had been explained to me I understood and I could put it into practice. Though in any new situation I still won't have a clue. I would need to do assertiveness training all the time and the training would have to be comprehensive, the type of training where everything is explained to you. As a child I was always waiting. I was waiting for an explanation. I kept wondering when they would finally explain how everything should be done. In the end, I just had to learn everything for myself, and anything I learn I can carry out perfectly.

Friends

As a child I always wanted to have friends. All children had friends and I wanted to have friends so I wouldn't feel excluded. But if anyone came up to me in the playground I was nasty to him or her because I couldn't handle it. What I really wanted was to be left alone all the time without any comments from anybody, because whenever another child came up to me I didn't know how to react. The other children knew this, and after a while they stopped coming up to me because my behaviour was weird and because I was different. Yet I really did want to have friends and play with other children, I just didn't know how. Social contacts only frustrated me and as a child I didn't know why. I didn't know what I was doing wrong. I didn't know what was different about me, which made things go wrong all the time. If only I could have had a friend, just one would have been enough. Then I wouldn't have felt so abnormal. The problem was that I did feel abnormal during such encounters. The other children looked at me, knowing full well that I was different.

Every now and then a friend used to come and play with me. One came because she was in love with my brother. Another one came because she could get me to do whatever she wanted. I had no real friends at primary school. Every time another child came home with me I didn't know how to play with them, so I just did whatever they asked. I didn't enjoy playing like that; I couldn't understand what the other children got out of it. Sometimes they played games of make-believe – I could never see the sense of that.

I was able to play with children that I knew well. I knew how they played and I knew what I had to do to join in. I learnt to play through imitation, because it didn't come naturally to me. When I had learnt I still couldn't play with other children who I didn't know very well, because I didn't know or understand their game. The few friends I had at primary school were girls who had sussed me out and more or less exploited it. After all, I was an easy playmate. They told me what to do and I complied without even thinking of moaning, as I was pleased to have finally found someone to play with. I thought I had made friends, but friendship had nothing to do with it – they were only using me for their games.

I still want to be able to socialise, but it scares me because I can't do it. In new situations I would prefer to be invisible. At the same time I want to prove to myself that I've got a diploma in social skills. It's very frustrating, making real contact with anyone is hard as it's so different every time. In fact, I always want to be left alone and not feel under pressure to socialise, but the need for genuine contact is enormous.

I can't make or maintain contacts normally in a relaxed way as I can't chat, I just don't understand informality. What also makes it tricky is that in certain situations (for example, with the Scouts) I can do a lot when somewhere else I can't. That has long confused me because I had no insight into the causes. I couldn't explain the big contrast. But now – since my diagnosis of autism – I know exactly why this is.

It scares me if I have no control over a situation; this makes me feel utterly powerless. I feel better in situations where I can decide – for instance where I can be the leader rather than a participant.

Structured activities are easier for me than other ones. During the informal period before a meeting starts, I feel awkward and self-conscious. Yet during the meeting itself I can usually handle myself quite well, often even better than the average participant, but only if the meeting is well structured, with a clear agenda and when people stick to the subject. I am very good at communicating when there is only one subject and I am aware of it.

After a meeting I usually try to get away as quickly as possible because I don't want to socialise. I can only cope with a few clearly defined contacts at most.

I have never really managed very well with colleagues. This is the reason why I keep changing my job or getting fired. Each time I get the same comments, "There are no problems with your work, but we don't know you, you're awkward, you're obstructing the team and your colleagues, nobody can get close to you, you don't anticipate, we have no idea what goes on in your mind..."

Making contacts

I am lucky enough to have a few close friends. All the same I notice that my contact with them is different from the contact between normal people. I still can't talk to them about serious matters in a normal way. Even if I can bring myself to tell them, I just can't communicate the right feelings. The feelings that I communicate do not reflect what I actually feel. I have to deduce how to get across what I feel and that isn't easy. Sometimes it seems as if I object to things when I don't and sometimes it's the other way round. I lack the insight and skill to let it happen naturally.

I can't make new friends; I have far too much trouble making contact. Friends in a group are also impossible, as my social skills are too poor. Often I don't even get on well with my best friends if we're in a group. I then feel as if I'm drowning in the social interactions of the group. They present far more information than I can process at the time and a large proportion of group interactions pass me by, so I can't join in.

I used to go on trips out with the Scouts or with friends and I was happy when I could go. Yet these were also the very nights when I was most unhappy. I saw other people chatting when I couldn't. I saw them interact on the dance floor, smiling and dancing, when I couldn't. I saw them making new contacts. I saw how someone kept trying to make contact with me but gave up because it didn't get him anywhere, even though there was nothing I would have loved more. I saw how I was part of a group of people but was excluded. I felt completely different and didn't know what was going on. I couldn't understand how other people did it and what I lacked that they had. It was often frustrating but I was still pleased when I could go on the trips. Then I 'went out' too. Going out meant sitting in a chair, listening to generally nice music, looking at people and dreaming how one day I might be able to talk to them. I felt very unhappy when I 'went out' but also learnt to love and enjoy it in a certain way. I needed to have the experience. I felt more normal if I could tell people I went out as well.

Physical contact is sometimes a problem. If something does not conform to my pattern, if something isn't right, or if the wrong word is used, then nobody is allowed to come near me or touch me. Sometimes I won't allow people to say anything at all, not even my boyfriend. If they do I will leave or sometimes hit or push them.

As a child I always tried to overcome this. I couldn't see any reason to shun physical contact. Now I know where it stems from and I understand, though that doesn't make it any easier to fight, as I just can't deal with it. My friends and other people around me feel this instinctively; they know that touching makes me feel uncomfortable. Even my best friends will hardly ever touch me – they never tap me on the shoulder or hug me.

When I was a Scout as a child there was a leader who was very popular. Every child competed for the honour of walking hand in hand with him. All day long I stayed near him so I could give him my hand and other children would see that I was also liked and that I was somebody. I desperately longed for that hand, because I missed contact a lot. I had very little emotional or physical contact with other people including the Scout leaders. On several occasions his hands were free during our walk and I was the only child near him. Yet I still didn't take his hand, even though I had been living for this moment all day. I had no idea how to go about it, how to grab hold of his hand. This was something that didn't come naturally to me and I didn't understand it. I felt so hurt and frustrated from then on that I never stayed anywhere near most of the leaders again. There was only one leader whose hand I was able to take. We wouldn't talk but just walked along in silence. Even now I don't shake hands with people if I can avoid it.

Whenever I'm sad or in pain I withdraw into myself. It never used to occur to me to seek comfort from someone else, and even now I still can't do it. I don't know how to ask to be comforted. I don't know what it's like to hug or to hold someone. I don't know how to tap someone on the shoulder or how to put a hand on someone's knee to comfort her. There is a lot I don't know. I can't do it, because it doesn't come naturally. I can't learn either, because other people sense that I'm not happy with it and therefore won't do it to me. Even my best friends don't hug me when I feel desperately unhappy or am crying.

At the Scouts there's a lad I get on well with. I enjoy the contact we have and I can chat easily with him. However, I have noticed that I can only do that in familiar surroundings and not anywhere else. Whenever I meet him in an unfamiliar setting communication becomes difficult. One day I went to the seaside with him. Before we left the Scout hut everything was fine. In the car there were no problems either, as we had been on car trips together before. But as soon as we got out of the car, all of a sudden from one moment to the next, things became strained simply because we were in a different setting. In a different situation things are no longer the same.

New people also cause me difficulties, as they unsettle me. This makes me feel ill at ease so I avoid any contact with them. Everything then immediately becomes more difficult. I'm thrown off balance in the presence of a new person. It takes a while before I can tolerate a new contact and have got used to them being there. I find new people threatening; they scare me and bewilder me. This causes me a lot of difficulties as a care worker. Sometimes it surfaces in ways I don't want. If there is a new trainee and my shift is over, then I'll say goodbye to everyone except the trainee. Or I will get drinks for everybody except the newcomer. I don't want this to happen but to me that person is still completely outside my world.

Eye contact

Eye contact can be a problem for me. I can make eye contact, but mainly with people that I know well. With people I don't know so well I can manage if there is someone else present that I feel safe and comfortable with. It's harder if I am on my own with someone I know and it's completely impossible with a stranger. I then come across as even more autistic. I wriggle my hands more, so people sometimes call me shy. But I'm not shy at all, I simply feel self-conscious. A new situation is tough and causes me a lot of stress, as I don't know how to behave.

Sometimes I wonder how successful I am with friends, because I get remarks from time to time. I was having a drink with my best friend. We were sitting in a pub and suddenly she said, "What's up with you? You're staring at me! Is there something wrong with my hair or is there a bit of food stuck between my teeth?" I was startled by her comment. I didn't mean to look and certainly not to gawk at her. This makes me feel uncertain. I begin to worry and then I don't know what to do anymore. In fact, I don't know what appropriate eye contact is.

Sometimes someone looks at me and I can't interpret that look. I can't see what goes on inside his head or what he means by a certain look. I often have the same problem with intonation. A certain intonation means that something is being said in an unusual tone. Mostly that is all there is to it. I then try to find out why he has said it in that particular tone rather than softer, louder, more resolutely or more composed. I can't understand any of it and can't interpret it. If someone touches me I often don't know how he or she means it, as I can't interpret that either. Because I genuinely 'feel' different – literally, that is – I have difficulty interpreting physical contact. As a result, I usually try to avoid it for fear of touching or looking at someone inappropriately or implying something I don't mean.

Conflicts

I have long been criticised unfairly during arguments and conflicts. Whenever I had a row with anyone I was invariably told it didn't even seem to bother me. They said I couldn't care less about the people around me and that I loved conflicts. For many years I had no idea where this accusation came from, I just didn't get it. I felt that I was trying hard to show that I did mind and was doing my best to make things right again. But I must have gone about it the wrong way, and although it was obvious to me it must have been confusing to others, which caused even more aggression or dissatisfaction.

After a row with someone it often goes quiet for a moment, when nothing is said or we keep our distance for a while. After two minutes I can walk up to that person again and start chatting about what I've been doing that day or about a TV programme I've seen. I can quite easily sit down next to him on the sofa, quite close. Or I can look at him and give him a happy smile. The other person will then usually get even angrier and start shouting that I couldn't care less about him, that I'm selfish, that I only make things more difficult and pretend that I don't care. Yet each time when this happened I felt I clearly showed that the argument wasn't all that bad, I genuinely did care about the other person and enjoyed his company and that our argument or conflict was not serious enough to spoil any further contact between us. I now realise how other people saw this, but at the time I had no other ways of showing it wasn't that bad and I forgave them. To me these were attempts at conciliation. I had no idea how I could have done it differently. I don't know how to make things right again or how you should make contact again. To me this was an obvious way, which unfortunately was misinterpreted.

When I say something I often use the same words as anyone else. Yet frequently people don't understand me or misinterpret my words. I can't adapt to situations and it seems that people say things differently in one situation compared to another. On top of that I often can't communicate my emotions efficiently or explain how I experience something. There is clearly a gulf between what I feel or think and how I put it across, and this is very annoying. If I want to say something when I feel sad, people sometimes congratulate me because they think I'm pleased; or the other way round. This makes me feel misunderstood. It gives me the impression that communication is restricting me, that communication is often pointless and that I can't communicate efficiently. Sometimes when I say something the other person understands me, then I'm pleased and say the same thing in the same way to someone else. Yet that person may not understand me, or I may come across quite differently because I have said it in a way that is inappropriate for the situation. For instance, when I'm answering a medical questionnaire I can state in a matter-of-fact way that I'm autistic. But it seems that when I told my parents about my diagnosis for the first time I needed to say this quite differently. I sometimes lack such insight and this can make me socially maladjusted. I say things in a way that is sometimes appropriate but at other times totally unacceptable. Sometimes I am understood and sometimes I am completely misjudged, which is not nice. Quite often I won't say anything for fear of being misunderstood or saying something inappropriate. Sometimes I need to think long and hard before I dare to say something fairly simple. Often I will first ask my boyfriend for an explanation. I will explain the situation in which I need to say something and ask him if that's acceptable. This extends my options somewhat. It would help if I could ask a few other people as well, but that is difficult.

My urge to communicate is limited. It frequently doesn't occur to me to announce something, but often an explanation is necessary when I want to talk about myself or if I want people to show me some consideration. Even then I usually don't communicate; if there is something I really don't want I may not make it clear.

Sometimes I find that strange myself, as it would solve many problems if I could be clearer. But the need to communicate is alien to me and I only bring something up when asked. Sometimes I simply wait for the question or I've got my answer ready in case a question comes up, which can cause difficulties.

For instance, one day the Scouts were going to help clear up after a church fete. I found this difficult to handle as it was too crowded and unpredictable, there were no permanent people for me to rely on and I simply lost track of the situation. I could have said to someone in the group that I couldn't help, but that didn't occur to me. So I just carried on without saying a word. In situations like that I then can't even bring myself to say 'hello'. Some people find this perplexing, while others get angry. I will then explain because I am asked to; of course, people ask me why I didn't say so before.

This happens with lots of things. I rarely tell other people about myself. In retrospect I usually intend to explain about myself a bit more in future. But still the problem keeps cropping up, time and time again because I don't communicate when necessary.

The same applies to asking for help. I will never ask anyone for help. I will never indicate when something is wrong or when I need something.

Meetings

Holding a conversation is difficult for me and there are a number of reasons for this. I can't cope with alternating between the roles of sender and receiver; getting the hang of this is tricky, because it keeps changing. Other people seem to manage it easily or are able to put this constantly changing perspective in its place. With me this doesn't happen automatically, and because I have no insight into it I often interrupt people. At the time I don't realise that it's inappropriate and I don't recognise when it is appropriate to say something. I have no sense of the space between words. I don't know when silences are part of the sentence or when they signal that it's the other person's turn to speak. I don't easily sense when I can interrupt a conversation, although I've learnt an awful lot and my interruptions are becoming subtler.

I'm much better dealing with people individually than in groups. If I try to talk to more than one person everything becomes too complicated for me. Getting to know people also happens on a one-to-one basis. Once I know someone another familiar person can join us, but I'd prefer it if this didn't happen.

I will often change the subject, which isn't very nice for the people I'm talking to. Again, I don't always realise it at the time, although I can sense it from the reactions of others. The problem is that I often get fixated on one particular word and go on about it. But I fail to see the context in which it was used and don't realise that by going on about it I will strip it of its context. For instance, a programmer might tell me that he has developed an interesting programme. I might suddenly take over the conversation and start talking about making candles, as I get stuck on the word interesting. After all, I find making candles an interesting hobby and so I just carry on from there. As a result, the conversation takes on a completely different direction.

I also find it difficult to give appropriate information when someone asks me a question. That's because I can't tell whether it is a big question, a minor question or just a question to show interest. Often I will explain in a short phrase when someone asks for detailed information and sometimes it's the other way round and I will explain in minute detail when in fact I am only asked about one small aspect. I will then start talking enthusiastically and will often drag other things into it that are completely irrelevant to that person. For instance, I might suddenly tell someone very intimate details when they only wanted to know if I live on my own.

At the same time I feel a great need for concrete, direct questions. If I am not asked any questions then I often don't know what to say. Questions provide structure in a conversation and clarify what needs to be said. Questions give direction, so that I don't drown in a mass of details. If I am asked about my childhood I am likely to say nothing. I just don't know where to start. I drown in the mass of details and can't categorise anything for myself. I can only do that if I'm asked specific questions that are not too broad in scope.

People frequently ask me two questions at the same time and then I may not answer because I'm not sure what the question is. I prefer unambiguous questions. I also find it difficult if something is said when someone is asking a question at the same time.

Chapter 8

Frustrations

If something is not right – the wrong word, a new situation, a change of plan or imagination or humour I don't understand – I react irritably, angrily and touchily and I feel defensive and full of reproach. I become self-tormenting and lose myself completely and feel that I need to impose an order. This is always triggered by a sense of powerlessness because I can't comprehend the world. Some people call them rages though to me that has nothing to do with it, but all the more with panic, powerlessness and fear.

People ask me a question and I can't answer, not because I don't know the answer but because I don't understand the question. They use the same words that I use, the same sentences, the same sentence structure, and yet to me the same sentence or question means something completely different. I interpret what they are saying literally which is wrong, because very few people mean exactly what they say. When I say something the world doesn't understand me, even if I say it a hundred times people still don't know exactly what I mean. I speak a different language to the rest of the world. The worst thing is that I can't learn other people's language, so that it will always be like this.

I want to be able to tell people that I really do speak a different language, that I don't understand them and that I really am different; it is not a case of unwillingness but rather of inability. I want people to recognise that. I want to be believed and to be able to be who I am at last. I need that for my own sake. This has caused me enough problems already. And for my own sake I want to know that I have tried hard enough to adapt, but that 'total' adaptation just isn't feasible. I want people to recognise that part of my identity as well. I don't want to be blamed all the time because I am different, and I want to be able to explain why that is. I don't want to keep fighting against disbelief all my life. I want to be able to be who I am.

I get the feeling that I constantly have to adapt to the world when I can't. I simply don't have the ability. I don't understand 'the' world and nobody understands 'my' world. I often get angry with myself and hope I will finally have learnt how to act and think differently. But that never happens. I want things to be different! I would give anything for it. But I can't do things differently. The links are missing. I think I lack the aptitude to understand the world; it simply isn't there. I feel that I will always live in a different world.

Taboo

Why do people regard autism as a taboo and treat me accordingly? Why does no one break the ice? Surely everyone knows there is something wrong with me; everyone talks about it but never with me, only with each other. Why do I always get the blame and the condemnation? Surely they must notice that there is a lot more to it and that I can't help it, however much I want things to be different? I'm not really a bad person. All the kids at school, at the Scouts, and at sports knew it, "Dominique is different, she is not like us." Everyone is aware and yet everyone keeps silent about it. No one brings it up, everyone acts as if everything is alright. I don't like that taboo.

I feel afraid in this world. It's as if you're on a journey to a very strange country. You don't know the language and everything is different: eating, working, dressing, sleeping, talking, and debating. I don't understand anything because I don't speak the language and no one talks to me. They do make gestures, but I don't understand a single one. They do exchange glances, but I don't understand a single one of those either. I will be afraid and unhappy all my life.

I have learnt things, but that doesn't mean I've taken them in. I only possess a rudimentary knowledge, like someone visiting a tribe of Indians in the Amazon jungle who has only read a book about them. You learn that they are people and that they eat a special kind of food, but that doesn't mean you understand their meals once you are with them. I can understand everything, but I don't comprehend it. I know I am always wrong but I can't manage to do and think the right thing. Other people also keep pointing out to me that I am wrong, and the fault lies with me and not with the world. I do realise that I should do things differently to be like everybody else. But even then I can't do it. If I do manage to resist, then there are always consequences for me: I feel powerless or I feel I need to pigeonhole everything.

I have difficulties dealing with feelings. I have many feelings – at least as many as anyone else and perhaps even more. So, although I am very sensitive, feelings also cause me a great deal of difficulty. I can't place my feelings. I often have them, but usually I don't understand where they come from or how to label them. I know about happiness and anger, but only in their most primitive forms, and any subtleties are beyond me. Anger is always more than just anger, happiness is always more than just happiness and sadness is always more than just sadness. My feelings of anger vary, and so do my feelings of happiness and sadness; they are never the same. And that is something I can't grasp or label. Generally, I can tell whether a feeling is positive or negative, although that is sometimes difficult too. I don't know what anger, happiness or sadness is exactly either. I put all the explanations together and try to understand it, but it remains tricky, as I can't truly grasp the words. Sometimes I have to describe to myself what is going on before I can try to attach a feeling to it on the basis of analysis. This is usually rather laborious and I have to think deeply to be able to label the feeling.

I've now learnt to use analysis and my emotional life has been a bit more organised since I started doing that. I am slowly learning and one day it may get easier. Labelling a feeling accurately is something I will probably never be able to do without rationalising it completely. I tend to reduce everything to a few feelings, because I don't possess the definitions of additional feelings. I can label very few feelings and even if I do label them, I still regularly get the feeling that it's not quite right, that the word doesn't quite cover the meaning. Usually, a feeling doesn't correspond to my definition of it and sometimes my definition is so broad that I can classify virtually anything under it. A positive feeling is often happiness; a negative feeling is often sadness.

All the various nuances seem like separate feelings to me. I experience them as such because I can't clarify them any further. To me, there are thousands of feelings that I can't grasp; consequently, I can't also be inundated by them. It would help if I could give them each a different name so I could get some insight into them. But unfortunately that is completely out of the question.

Intelligence

Sometimes I wish my intellectual abilities were much more limited. I now have enough to realise that I am different and so I have to behave accordingly – I have to hide that I'm different. As a result I feel frustrated most of the time when I'm with other people. Sometimes I prefer to be alone as that is easiest.

When I lose my temper because something is wrong I know that is abnormal and I have to look for a more acceptable form of expression. When I was a child, there were fewer inhibitions. I used to feel just as unhappy or perhaps even more so. But life would be much simpler if I could just let go whenever something was wrong, if I could just scream or become hysterical rather than experience so much powerlessness, anger and chaos inside me because of the incomprehension.

When I was a child everything was more difficult and at the same time a lot easier. It was more difficult because I was flooded with impressions and experiences that I couldn't identify. As a child I understood even less of what was going on. Also, I had fewer means of communication, although sometimes that actually made it easier. I had no real, efficient way to communicate, but because I was a child this was tolerated. Now no one will tolerate it anymore, and people expect more from me. I look normal and so people expect me to communicate properly as well. They expect me to express problems or ask questions in a reasonable and acceptable manner.

I have noticed that people with autism who are weaker are often better or more transparent at refusing something than stronger people. Often I am unable to refuse something and that is usually because there are so many other things involved. If a weaker young person couldn't drink from a yellow cup he could just push it aside. But if I am offered a yellow cup and I really don't want to drink from it, then I know that it is not acceptable behaviour and therefore I don't dare to refuse or push the cup aside. People simply don't notice anything odd about me, so they expect me to function normally. I know that not wanting to drink from a yellow cup is actually very silly, and the realisation that the problem lies within me because I'm different is then so overwhelming it is impossible for me to refuse – even if I know it would ruin my whole day. The urge to be seen as 'normal' plays a strong part and I long to be like others; I often don't refuse because I don't want to be the odd one out. I do my very best to keep up with others, but it does take its toll when you are confronted – often in a cruel way – with being different and when you're completely misunderstood all the time. I want to be like other people and if that means I have to drink from a yellow cup then I will try to do so, even if I know how serious the consequences may be to myself.

Of course I often don't know how to refuse. Even if I try to say so clearly it sounds so awkward that people will find it very odd and will certainly not be sympathetic. How do you say that you don't want to drink from a yellow cup? How do you say that to someone who doesn't know anything about your autism or about autism in general?

As a child everything was still more or less possible. In a letter from the Centre for Psychological, Medical and Social Services I was described as a difficult, headstrong child who was irascible. I asked my mother what irascible meant. To me, that letter was proof that I was different and I have always wondered – and still do – why nobody has ever brought it out into the open. After all, everybody knew about it, didn't they? It is a constant struggle for me and often I can't manage it. Even now there are frequent tantrums, rages and irritable and touchy reactions. There is a lot of yelling, screaming, pigeonholing and self-punishment. To others I still seem very touchy, intolerant and illogical, or the opposite: apathetic, detached, not participating and unable to make contact. According to others I have no tolerance for frustration and I always have to have it all my way. But to me that isn't true. There is always a reason! I don't understand the world and that's why I behave oddly.

If I had fewer abilities I would no doubt have to cover up less. I may have been an awkward problem child, but now I spend too much energy on acting as normal as possible and on reacting to things that seem impossible to me. All my life I have had the feeling that I am to blame for all kinds of things that are not my fault. I am sometimes difficult because I don't understand anything. Does that make me guilty?

Different

I have always had the feeling that people don't appreciate that I am different. Although they won't ignore me, they won't truly accept me either. They think I'm odd and don't want to accept my oddness. I am different and being different is exceptional. What's more, they don't look at how I am instead; I'm just atypical. It seems as if they don't want to make any allowances at all. They either laugh with me or ignore it completely and rarely bring it up. I have one friend who does, though. He is a special friend who just tells me that he finds me very odd, that I talk weird, that I'm very feebish (autistic). Whenever I do or say something autistic – i.e. when I do something he finds stupid – he will tell me. He finds it funny that I'm so silly. He also laughs at me to my face whenever I act strange. But he does it in such a way that it doesn't feel like jeering. Although it may sound strange, it's more as if he accepts it. He just lets it be and doesn't mind the way I am. He compares me to the Phoebe character from the American TV series *Friends*. Many people would find that highly insulting but it's not meant like that. To me it is acceptance – something that I experience very rarely. Whenever I do something feebish he yells the name 'Phoebe'. He is the only one who admits that I'm very feebish. This makes me feel as if my autism is perfectly acceptable.

Had people known about my autism when I was a child, then I would have had the right support and I would have developed a lot further in some respects. On the other hand, I am glad that I wasn't diagnosed until much later. I am happy that things have turned out this way. While I may not have had a lot of understanding or the right support, I did get many chances. My parents could never refuse me anything just because of my autism, as they didn't know about it I was able to go into mainstream education and then on to study Educational Science. I'm delighted that I was given that chance, which I probably wouldn't have had if they had known about my autism. The course helped to turn me into the kind of person I am now; I would never have been so open or so assertive without it. It has made me stronger and I have had to fight hard to achieve something for myself. I am really grateful for that.

I'm learning to be more aware of my autism. If people tell me something I try to translate it by asking myself straight away if whatever was said could perhaps be meant differently. Sometimes this helps me to realise sooner where things go wrong. Nevertheless, even then it is often too late. I long to join in so much that I will often try to anticipate possible difficulties. Despite all my efforts I simply cannot prevent all autistic incidents. It's a shame that it demands so much energy and exhausts me so much that I can never keep it up for long although I always try my very best. If only I could show how much effort it takes me, people would surely understand me a lot better and then they wouldn't blame me or give me any more funny looks. Living with autism hurts a lot, especially when you are with other people who are not autistic. Because they provide such a big contrast they make the pain so much worse.

One day I told my parents that autism is part of me and that I refused to be silent for their sake. I said that I was going to live my life the way I want to and that I would talk about autism whenever I want and whenever I need to. I told them they had better accept it and put up with it. If they find it difficult then that's too bad, but I'm the one who has to live with it. I could only deal with it by talking about it. I have kept quiet for too long, I have kept myself hidden away for too long. Hidden away from everyone, in my desire to be normal or at least to seem normal, ever since I've known there was something wrong. From now on I'll stand up for myself and fight my corner and I will not give up. I will not put up with people who feel I should shut up or with people who doubt my diagnosis. After all my suffering and feeling misunderstood all my life, I have finally accepted it. It's now up to other people to accept it as well. If they find it hard I will be the first to understand. But after the long road I've travelled I feel they should meet me at least some of the way. I will not keep hiding; I will not carry on suffering. I feel that my request to others to accept it is no big deal. All they have to do is listen to my story – I have had to live through it, whereas other people only need to hear how dreadful it is to me. All I ask of others is to believe me.

My psychiatrist recently stressed that I need to stop trying to make other people understand me all the time. He told me that other people will never understand me completely and that there would always be a gap. I would only become frustrated if I continued to push myself so much. He said that other people should also do their share and meet me halfway and that I am doing my bit. My explanations are sufficient and other people should make the effort to start trying to understand me. He says it should come from both sides and that I should be satisfied with that. I have now reached the stage where I am able to do that to some extent. If I am to make any further progress, others will now have to take some steps in my direction.

The efforts I make are sometimes enormous, and yet I always feel I could do more, that I could have given that little bit of additional information. In that respect I am still looking for a state of equilibrium.

I have fought for a diagnosis because it clarifies a great deal. Because I want to say that I really am different and because I want to be able to explain what makes me different. I thought people would feel more sympathy or at least understand me better. But I keep experiencing a great lack of understanding: people who brush aside any problems, refuse to show me any consideration or don't even take the time to hear what my problem is.

All this may seem overwhelming and sad, and in a way it is, especially in unfamiliar situations. But I have learnt to cope and can function fairly normally in some of those conditions. In some ways I do realise what is normal and what isn't. I hide, cover up and counteract a lot. Most people don't notice the contact that falters. People who see me on a daily basis or who know me well notice a lot more: the social contacts, communication and language, the tantrums, the planning... Autism is within. I can feel it and I feel it bloody hard, all the time and wherever I am.

My autism often makes me feel very unhappy. It is tough to be confronted all the time with having no hold over anything and being unable to take part in the world. Now that I've got a diagnosis I regularly think things will improve but in fact it can be even more difficult.

I still need to learn how to explain it to others so that I can ask for more understanding, but I haven't reached that stage yet. I still cannot put my autism into words properly; it's still too early for that. I'm still not clear about it myself and can't quite grasp it yet. I hope that one day I will find my way.

E.T. (again)

People don't get through to me. They walk up to me, but never reach me. There is always some distance, always a wall they cannot get past and neither can I, because I'm stuck behind the wall. I can't escape, I'm imprisoned in my own head and I can't get away. Each time all my efforts achieve nothing and I feel that people are turning against me. The wall is not going to be pulled down and never will be. I'm imprisoned in my head and will stay there. I will never escape. I want to get rid of my head. I want to escape. I want to abandon it. I want to be free. It restricts me too much. I don't understand the world. I can't see any structures; everything is chaos. I only partly understand myself. I wish I had someone who could accompany me, so that I didn't have to travel by myself. I'm afraid on my own and nobody takes me by the hand through that big, incomprehensible, dangerous world. Everything scares me; the things I have to do on my own fill me with dread. Nobody ever really comes close to me. I will always be different. Inside I will always feel different. I am alone, quite alone, and that hurts. The wall cannot come down. It stays there. Forever.

Sometimes people tell me that I look just like anybody else. But that's only on the outside. Inside, in my head, I'm E.T. and the problem is that it's impossible to look inside my head. People don't get through to me. All the same I long for real contact with another human being. If I want them to know something about me, I will have to go to them, as they cannot get to me. I will always have to take that road on my own, because there is nobody to accompany me. There is no gate that leads inside of me. If I want to share I will have to go outside and then I will either reach a man of stone or a person with a heart. That's the way it is for me. Sometimes they will listen to me, but sometimes they won't. Even so, my words are the same and I speak the same language. I use exactly the same sentences. Damn! Why does it not get across sometimes? Sure, now and then I shut myself away, because I feel too much. It wouldn't be so bad if I could share, but what if I reach the man of stone again?

Yet the man of stone doesn't exist while at the same time he is everyone else. The problem of the stone lies with me and with nobody else. Some days I manage to speak the same language and then it's the person with a heart. But another time if I say exactly the same thing to someone else, then it's a man of stone. And when I talk to a man of stone he still seems like a person with a heart, because the difference between the stone and the heart lies within me. One day my language will be understood, but not the next. Some days I sense how to say something and be understood; I am then talking to a person with a heart. But next time I won't sense how to say something and then I'm talking to a man of stone. I often feel hurt when I talk to a man of stone. But I'm guilty of it myself. I can't help it. I'm E.T. and can't fathom the language of Earth.

I'm terribly lonely and the fact that people don't come near me makes me very sad. I regret this and sometimes find it hard to understand that the cause lies with me, because I try my very best and it's my greatest desire to establish real contact. Yet I keep failing. Although I understand it, it is still hard to accept because it cannot be helped. I can't change anything – that's the way it is and always will be.

I'm somewhere else but I can't say where I am. There is no road that leads towards me. I will never be found and can't get away either. I feel as if I don't come from Earth but from another planet. I don't belong here. I'm not at home here. I'm a counter magnet. It's not easy to say this but that's how it feels.

How else can I explain what I am like? I only wish people could see inside my head. Then they could see what makes me tick. Then they wouldn't find me so bizarre anymore. Everything is so atypical, so different.

To me it's as if there's always a war going on, everywhere and all the time. I'm constantly in conflict with the whole world. There are always clashes. The worst is that I'm in a minority. I always lose.

I don't understand the world and the world doesn't understand me. I'm angry at the world and the world is angry with me. I'm not allowed to be a part of the world, but I still fight for the privilege, even though I know I will never win. I'm different and there's no room for me. The harder I try, the more frustrated I get. I will always be separate from the rest. I will remain separate from that big, unattainable world. I will stay on my own planet.

A Positive Conclusion

People sometimes ask me if there are any positive aspects to having autism. There certainly are, for instance, frankness. I am very frank in my dealings with people. It never occurs to me to express anything differently just because it may need to come across differently. I can't see the point of that. I use words for the purpose for which they are intended: to tell the truth. Many people use words differently. They don't come to the point. Ask them what they are thinking and often they will not say what they are thinking at all. I don't understand why people are so evasive. I don't understand why they regularly want other people to think their views are different from what they really believe. To me that is proof of insincerity and a sign that something is wrong. Such people are vague because I can no longer understand them.

Honesty

If there is something I object to or dislike then I'll just say so. I don't care if that flies in the face of someone else's opinion. Why should I butter them up? To my mind, a totally different opinion is just as good as the same one. If people are frank it doesn't matter to me what they are saying, whether it's rude or not.

I'm equally straightforward in my dealings with other people. If someone does something I cannot bear, then I have no qualms about saying so. If someone has upset me or if I feel that someone is rude to me or shows no respect, then I can just tell that person. I love dealing with people who wear their heart on their sleeve. That's exactly how I treat people or at least people that I know and trust. I only feel at ease with them if I can do that. When this is not tolerated I don't feel secure enough to be myself. I then clam up and say very little because I'm afraid to talk. I then feel that people don't speak my language. That's the way I am and my autism simply leaves me no alternative.

This is also quite obvious during arguments. Arguments seldom concentrate on the issues but are about petty details. Nevertheless, those trivialities become the focus of the argument when in reality they are not. During an argument I come straight to the point. That can be awkward for some, although usually people appreciate it. This is also the reason why I enjoy socialising with other people who have autism. They can suddenly say something that might be tough to other people but that I understand perfectly and am pleased to hear. For instance, one day an autistic acquaintance of mine was playing on the computer. He asked if I would come and have a look. I followed his game and suddenly he said, "Go away, because with you here I'm not playing as well anymore." Other people would not have appreciated his boldness or would have interpreted it as unfriendly, but I didn't. To me such behaviour is plain and therefore understandable. It's my language, it's the way my world is organised and that's the way I like it. I do understand that some things should be phrased carefully because it might be a touchy subject, but I cannot understand why you should then say something completely different.

Talks

My talks on autism are part of my personal coping mechanism. Talking about it does me good; it helps me to work everything out and to learn to live with the diagnosis better. But I also do it for other people with autism, hoping they will draw some comfort from my story. I also do it for anyone who thinks they are autistic, so they can finally give a name to their feelings and experiences over the years. So that things become clearer to them, when there is an explanation that helps them find their way. So they no longer feel alone in the world, knowing there are others like them, hoping that they will seek help or will reach out and may find sympathy from the people around them. But above all I give talks for all those with autism who are unable to explain or say what it is, what it means and how they feel.

I also talk about it with friends or with people who want to know more. Just talking about it is getting easier. I can then make it clear to other people what having autism means to me and what it's like to live with; they tend to be fascinated by it. But I can only manage it if I feel it's the right place and there is enough time.

Living with others

People who read this account may get the impression that I'm impossible to live with. But, like anybody else, I go to work, have a relationship, hobbies and friends. People who don't know about my autism never notice it when they see me from a distance or know me only vaguely. I am quite capable. I can manage reasonably well and on the whole I'm happy with my life. I know plenty of people on whose support I can count. They help me with my plans, teach me to be solution-minded and to break down patterns that are based on the wrong connections. I have people I can ring if things become too much for me or if I can't make any sense of a situation.

Some people wonder how anybody can live with someone like me. People who ask this question are reversing the situation. That's a different matter altogether. Living with me is fine; living in society is the difficulty. I try my very best to carve myself a place in this society and to learn some of its rules. But it's like installing a computer programme written in a different computer language. It's not compatible and you cannot make it compatible either. You don't use diesel components in a car that runs on petrol. But in itself I have no problems. In itself everything is fine. I have no difficulty socialising! Drop me on a desert island, without this society, without all these rules, and I have no difficulties. If everyone were autistic my autism wouldn't be a handicap. The world would be a much nicer place for me if everyone were autistic. So-called normal people would then be autistic, because our order would dominate while the other order would be deviant. A different order might therefore have been just as likely – one where words are taken literally, where people do as they say and where façades would disappear. Would it make a strange world, the one in which I feel at home?

I am only seen as abnormal when I socialise with other people. Why? Because I don't conform to the conventional picture. A picture created by the majority and which the majority decides is normal. But what is normal? If someone tells me he will ring me in ten minutes and I get angry when he still hasn't rung after twelve, then I'm wrong and he is right, because I'm autistic and he is normal. Someone has written a text and asks for my honest opinion. I am honest and say I think the piece is bad. Nevertheless I am wrong, he is right, I'm autistic, he is normal. Someone asks me how I am. I reply, "Terrible". The conversation is over because I should have said, "Fine", because it was only intended as an opening phrase. Still I am wrong, he is right, because I'm autistic and he is normal.

Can anybody tell me how the world of normal people is structured? Why am I not allowed to be punctual? Why can't I be honest? Why do people ask questions when they already know the answers? What is more logical than being autistic? People don't say what they mean and that is supposed to be normal. Once I've got the hang of it I can view myself as more normal. I've got a lot to learn. I will start by learning to lie and by not using words as they are intended.

Fortunately, normal people also include some difficult people. Long live the normal person who wears his heart on his sleeve. Everybody else finds him rude and difficult, but not me. Long live the normal person who is pernickety and who does look at his watch when he says he is expecting a phone call in seven minutes. How I hate not understanding such things that seem to be so simple for most people. How I hate my autism. But how I love those rare moments in my life when people appreciate me precisely because of these things. At times like that they almost make me feel proud. How happy I am when my friends are pleased about my frankness and when they are my friends for that very reason. How happy I am when my fellow human beings appreciate my honest opinion. How happy I am when it pleases other people that I am so punctual.

Children

My autism is a major trump card in my contact with children and adolescents. All children and adolescents need clarity and structure. This creates feelings of safety and trust. I am convinced that in some respect my autism makes me an excellent care worker, leader and guide. I am one of the Scout leaders and enjoy the authority and respect of the kids. Children know that I do as I say. They know the boundaries that I indicate. As a result, I get on very well with children and can give them confidence; I often get a lot out of them. I also regularly deal with children who are more difficult than the average child, and with them I certainly notice that my frankness pays off. I can usually control them fairly quickly. Children feel at ease with me. Since I was often unjustly blamed as a child myself I feel it's important to have a positive approach towards children. I acknowledge them and let them believe in themselves. I point out to them what they are doing well and always try to take them seriously.

Touching

I am reasonably advanced in my social contacts, especially outwardly. These contacts are based on learnt behaviour rather than on any real communication. Like someone who could reel off a theory by heart but has no idea what it's about and couldn't apply it. I know the surface; I have mastered the outer layer. But what really lies below the surface remains a mystery to me. Having mastered the superficial I am able to achieve a great deal, precisely because to some extent it can be comprehended and explained rationally. This also allows me to apply it; I simply do as I'm told. Social skills' training is therefore useful, since everything is explained and you are even allowed to practise and experiment. But there are also limits. Apparently not all aspects of social contact can be put into sentences and words. Not everything can be understood rationally, least of all the deeper dimensions in feelings and in what happens between people. I do have feelings, but I don't sense the rules that apply to other people.

There is a difference between feeling (which works fine) and sensing. Sensing is much more difficult. It assumes that you are able to interpret a large proportion of someone else's behaviour; this is the difficulty. Apparently such things are often put into unspoken rules. These are things that everybody knows, but I don't feel them because my norms are different. Even the feeling itself has a kind of literalness, a skirting round the issues. To other people, however, they are self-evident unchangeable facts. I find this difficult. Contact with me will never be the way it is with other people, precisely because the naturalness is lacking and precisely because the contact is based on learnt behaviour rather than the result of personal growth or my awareness.

I do feel that something is right or wrong. I also feel a bond between myself and certain other people. But to some degree I don't sense how certain things should be done in order to comply with the rules of the majority; there is a social ambiguity. The rules can be learnt for many things, but not all.

Contact has many dimensions, touching is one of them. But with almost all my contacts there is no touching. It does happen with my boyfriend, and it usually also happens with children, older people and the mentally handicapped in my role as a care worker. With them I can manage it, but not with anybody else. I will never ever touch anybody spontaneously. I cannot touch people as I don't know how to. Patting someone on the back, holding someone's hand, stroking someone, getting hold of someone to comfort him or her... I never do that. The absence of physical contact sometimes disturbs a relationship and it can hamper any deepening of feelings. The lack of physical contact often gives me the feeling that I am not capable of genuine contact. It creates a distance between myself and other people; it frustrates me and leaves me disheartened. Not being able to touch is a bit like being deaf or blind.

As a Scout leader I was in charge of a girl with autism. She enjoyed herself at the youth club. She said little but did indicate when she had a genuine difficulty with something, although I usually had to make the first move. It was difficult to figure her out. She found touching difficult, too. At one point we were playing a game that required a certain degree of physical contact. We were afraid she would refuse this. But suddenly – as part of her game – she got hold of a leader. Suddenly she made physical contact. She had discovered how she could be physical with that leader. This opened up a whole new world for her. She blossomed. From then on she was the one to make contact, came to tell us her story and just took us by the arm if she felt the need. She finally began to learn how to hold someone by the arm and how to touch someone. Her autism remained obvious but the contact with her was totally different. Suddenly she knew how to touch. She flourished and was suddenly no longer quiet.

Recently, something similar happened with Roger, a coach at (W)underway. We were playing. I stood in the doorway and Roger was not allowed to pass. Unintentionally, I grabbed hold of him to stop him. Later on I was again able to touch him. Because of this incident Roger became very special to me. He gave me a beautiful gift. Roger freed me. He tore down the walls around me one by one. He can walk straight up to me and I can walk up to him. It makes me feel good. I feel as if I'm recovering from something I could never do before but which I am now suddenly able to do. I can finally have normal physical contact with some people, spontaneously without having to rationalise it. Touching becomes enjoyable, and I want to touch whereas before I used to avoid it, as I didn't know how to; touching was a foreign language that I couldn't understand. It is a liberating feeling. That's why I enjoy being near Roger – at last a contact that is enjoyable and not just frustrating. It gives me energy.

Love

Some people are amazed when I mention that I am in a relationship. My boyfriend Bart and I spend a lot of time together. First I must explain that my boyfriend is truly fantastic to me. He really understands my autism and me. By that I mean that he sees the effect that autism has on me. We often talk about it, so he knows how it drains me, frustrates me and often makes me feel dejected. However, his understanding is purely rational. Any real insight into what I feel is impossible, but we get quite far with rational understanding alone. Bart is very close to me in that respect. I feel that he really understands me, even though he will never be able to get down to the heart of the matter. But that isn't necessary, as I can explain everything about my autism to him. Nothing is too silly or too stupid or too bizarre. He is open to everything and is always prepared to listen to everything with the same degree of willingness, understanding and patience. He can listen to me for hours. He will try to take it on board and will often look for a parallel. Such parallels usually help us out. Sometimes he uses an image to explain how he understands it. I will then say what is wrong about it and then he will adjust the image or will look for another one. We can go on like this for hours. He never gets bored. He keeps listening and patiently trying to understand me.

Bart also keeps distinguishing between my autism and my character. That way he finds it easier to deal with me, and it enables him not to take it too personally if I'm being awkward again. He realises that it's my autism and therefore does not get angry (unlike nearly everybody else!) but immediately wants to help me. He knows there is something wrong with my plans, the words are wrong; there is too much imagination or not enough concrete language. He will then help me look for solutions to make everything alright again. He does that time and time again with the same amount of patience. I can be screaming and shouting, but he will run to my aid looking for answers and solutions. He will then comfort me ever so gently and tell me that I don't need to apologise.

It was not always like this. Before I had been diagnosed, Bart couldn't put up with me ranting and raving; he found my behaviour very unreasonable and even got really angry with me. We always ended up having flaming rows. A few times we nearly broke off the relationship, but each time we decided to give it another try; our love was too great. But we were very worried about my unreasonable moods. We both knew that something serious was going on but didn't know what. After the diagnosis everything fell into place and it all started to make sense. We realised that all our rows could be reduced to my autism. As a result, our understanding grew and the rows soon disappeared. Now such moments of doubt about our relationship have gone completely. There are no more crises. It has made our relationship much simpler and stronger. If ever we do argue we usually manage to patch things up pretty quickly. We keep talking until we understand each other again and are back on the same wavelength.

Apart from that my boyfriend is very tolerant, even though I do things that are illogical. He lets me have my way. He also fits in with all my whims. Sometimes my autism puts me at risk of losing my grip in certain situations. I then usually plan all sorts of things to control myself again. I do the dishes, go shopping, etc. Bart always understands how important this is to me and cooperates with my whimsical behaviour.

Bart loves me and accepts my autism. He doesn't see it as an obstacle but loves me partly because of my autism. I often say that I wish I wasn't autistic. Bart frequently replies that we might then never have been a couple. So to some extent he also loves my autism. Bart appreciates its positive aspects and there are only a few people who can manage that. There are not many people who look at me the way Bart does. He has found a girlfriend who is special. He refers not only to the autism but also to my character, my behaviour, the understanding that I show. It pleases him that I enjoy the little things that other people ignore. I draw his attention to things that would otherwise have escaped him: colours, sounds and smells. When walking through a park with me Bart always says that it's not the same park anymore. He feels that I constantly give him precious gifts because of my autism.

Epilogue
By Theo Peters

When I began to develop an interest in autism, some thirty years ago, I read through international scientific literature. In those days it was not very extensive but it taught me a great deal. Nevertheless I only discovered a new dimension to autism once I started talking to parents. That was 'live' autism.

Now, so many years later, I feel a similar 'Aha' experience when talking to people with autism and high intelligence (or people with Asperger's Syndrome), particularly when I read their books – those by Donna Williams, Temple Grandin, Gunilla Gerland... and now Dominique Dumortier. Through these books I get to know autism from within.

Many people who get to know someone with autism and high intelligence experience a kind of culture shock, as if people from two different cultures meet. They are privileged moments that occur only rarely in your life. It is as if you sense intuitively that from then on your life will be different somehow, that you will have to change certain types of understanding, and that from now on you will have to view autism from a different perspective. This feeling came over me when I got to know Gunilla Gerland better. She was able to give herself and her life a place in this world after she had read psychology books and realised she had autism, a diagnosis that was later confirmed by the medical world. Even though it came very late, this discovery was a great relief to Gunilla.

It may seem far-fetched to many people that someone might actually want a diagnosis of autism, but people with autism often experience this: they are desperately looking for their own identity. Dominique Dumortier, too, was delighted with her diagnosis. Thanks to the diagnosis she finally knew why she was 'different'. This recognition reminds me of an interview the neurologist Oliver Sachs had with Temple Grandin. He asked her if she wouldn't like to be 'normal' and she replied, "If I could snap my fingers and would be normal instantly, I wouldn't do it, because I wouldn't be myself. Autism is part of who I am."

Gunilla Gerland, too, once gave the following response when asked if she wouldn't like to be 'normal', "Maybe for a week or so, to know what it's like, but then I'd want my autism back again."

The same applies to Dominique, who like those mentioned above, was diagnosed as an adult. She does not regard the label of autism as a condemnation but rather as a release. To many people the diagnosis of autism is essential in order to get their personal integration going. Once they know they've got autism they no longer need to struggle to appear 'normal' or perform tricks they've learnt in order to meet the expectations from 'our culture'.

I am very pleased that Dominique Dumortier has had the courage to tell her story. It describes how she is trying to survive amongst 'ordinary people' – it's a tremendous adventure.

We 'teach' people with autism, we help them, but we can also learn a great deal from them. I feel this is a major challenge over the next decades: can we listen to them sufficiently and can we collaborate with them to build up any real integration? Not the naïve integration model in which we see ourselves as the criterion for any quality of life (after all, our standard is 'being normal', isn't it?) but one in which we see there are multiple forms of quality of life that deserve every respect.

Of course, people with autism need us, because otherwise they can't survive among us, but we also need their help for a better understanding of autism, to develop a different way of being together, respectful of their otherness.

Dominique's book speaks for itself. She too tells about the need for genuineness, for acceptance, the longing for a harmonious coexistence with others, even though she will always remain on her planet. It is not a question of reluctance but of inability. We (the so-called normal people) have the same problems when trying to get into the minds of people with autism. But we have made progress, slowly but surely.

Gunilla Gerland herself once expressed this beautifully in a fax to me. After her talks at the Autism Training Centre I took her back to the airport. On the way there I remarked that she used quite a few literary expressions, humour too and terms with a double meaning, in short she used a fair amount of 'NT speak' ('neurotypical language'). I faxed her about this and received the following reply:

In any case, nowadays I am able to use quite a bit of NT speak and I feel (paradoxically) I am growing closer to the NT culture the more I read about autistic culture. In my mind's eye I see this image of two cultures (autistic and NT) as two gardens with a fence in between.

Some people are able to walk up to the fence and talk to the people from the other culture, but other people are still too far away from the fence. I often see myself sitting on the fence, sometimes with someone sitting next to me, although that is rare. Nevertheless there is plenty of room on the fence.

But more and more people from both cultures are walking towards the fence to talk to each other and I think it's wonderful.

Talks by Dominique Dumortier can be arranged with:

Opleidingscentrum Autisme vzw
Plantin en Moretuslei 12
2018 Antwerp
Belgium
TEL +32 3 235 37 55
FAX +32 3 236 58 46
info@ocautisme.be

Contact address for Dominique Dumortier:
van_een_andere_planeet@yahoo.com

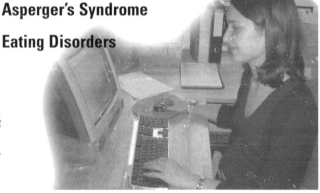